How to Write

How to Write

Alastair Fowler

OXFORD
UNIVERSITY PRESS

OXFORD
UNIVERSITY PRESS

Great Clarendon Street, Oxford OX2 6DP

Oxford University Press is a department of the University of Oxford.
It furthers the University's objective of excellence in research, scholarship,
and education by publishing worldwide in

Oxford New York

Auckland Cape Town Dar es Salaam Hong Kong Karachi
Kuala Lumpur Madrid Melbourne Mexico City Nairobi
New Delhi Shanghai Taipei Toronto

With offices in

Argentina Austria Brazil Chile Czech Republic France Greece
Guatemala Hungary Italy Japan Poland Portugal Singapore
South Korea Switzerland Thailand Turkey Ukraine Vietnam

Oxford is a registered trade mark of Oxford University Press
in the UK and in certain other countries

Published in the United States
by Oxford University Press Inc., New York

British Library Cataloguing in Publication Data
Data available

Library of Congress Cataloging in Publication Data
Fowler, Alastair.
  How to write / Alastair Fowler.
    p. cm.
  Includes bibliographical reference and index.
  ISBN-13: 978-0-19-927850-3 (alk. paper)
  ISBN-10: 0-19-927850-4 (alk. paper)
1. English language—Rhetoric.   2. Report writing.   I. Title.
  PE1408.F548 2006
  808'.042—dc22   2006008853

Typeset by RefineCatch Limited, Bungay, Suffolk
Printed in Great Britain
on acid-free paper by
Clays Ltd., St Ives plc

ISBN 978-0-19-927850-3 (Pbk.)

4

Preface

This is not a writing manual, nor a guide to grammar, nor to rhetoric. Obviously not: look at its length, or lack of it. It is only a small book aiming to help you form ideas about writing, and to write whenever you want to. Writing need not be an ordeal nor an impossible feat. It is a do-able task: one that becomes a pleasure when you get into it.

Reading this book should make writing easier, and should keep you from breaking your head in attempts on the impossible. But I don't guarantee masterpieces. In fact, I don't mean to deal with creative writing. How could one ever generalize about the ways of creative writers? Their methods are individual to a fault: some pursue total spontaneity; some mull over poems for months and then write them in a day; while Georges Simenon wrote within the same timetable as his story. This book merely tells how to write to a deadline, without fuss, pieces like reports, essays, term papers, or theses, with a more or less predetermined size. Some of this may be of interest to poets, novelists, and those who would like to be one or the other; but that is purely coincidental.

Writing an assignment to a deadline may seem simple enough. But forty years' reading of students' papers of various sorts, in both the UK and the USA, has taught me otherwise. Some papers were cobbled together without discernible signs of planning, and obviously written at the last moment. Others were out of scale, or dealt with only part of the assigned topic. A few were missing altogether ('I just couldn't get started'): the non-writer had waited for inspiration that never came. Yet this was not always due to laziness or lack of motivation. On the contrary, some students had done far too much preparatory reading (as one could tell from their opening paragraphs of agonized methodological wrestling) or had over-revised and prematurely polished a faulty argument. I infer there is a place for some such book as this. Indeed, it arose out of lectures that were repeated by request.

Why do so many people—not only students—have problems with writing? The historical reasons can be briefly given. Until the early nineteenth century, educated people could apparently write whenever they wanted to, by using one rhetorical method or another. But then, formal rhetoric became perhaps too rule-bound. In any case it was rejected—to be replaced by expressive writing. People began to wait for inspiration: for overflows of powerful feeling which sometimes moved them to write but often didn't. There is no going back to the old rhetoric. It depended on arts of memory and on a knowledge of the classics now beyond recovery. Instead, we need a different, more informal rhetoric: one based on a modern grammar closer to speech yet with the exactness and nuances of written language. And we need a method of writing such as will allow for precise distinctions, when these are appropriate, as well as for easy serendipities—'I don't know what I mean to say until I say it.'

We have been through a phase of education when grammar was ignored and writing thought possible without it: a phase when spelling, and therefore distinction between words, was neglected; when it was thought 'too discouraging' for a teacher to correct errors. Some people feel deprived by this, and want to catch up. This book is meant partly for them.

I shall say little about style, because for ordinary writers image is not everything—is in fact, compared to function, very little. The focus will be on how to make words work. Robert Lanham claims that 'America is the only country in the world rich enough to have the leisure, and democracy enough to have the inclination, to teach its whole citizenry not merely to write, but to write well.' In my view, no country can afford *not* to do this, for the sake of simple efficiency, let alone the quality of life.

The chapters that follow need not be read in any one sequence. It's all right to jump ahead to what seems more interesting, or back to what you passed over at first. Readers' needs are so various that a mosaic structure seemed best. With this in mind, I have supplied an index and have sometimes given cross-references (in small capitals) to other chapters.

Writing manuals are usually designed for a specific readership. But this is a book for several sorts of reader, from beginners to senior citizens: all those, indeed, who sometimes have to write but find it difficult. Inevitably, then, some of the book will not be right for you. If you find a section irrelevant to your needs, too easy or obscure, simply move on. Use the Index, or browse: you may find another section that speaks to you. To save time, the book is bluntly phrased. But I don't mean to be unnecessarily prescriptive: there are many different ways of writing, and if the way I suggest provokes you to practise its opposite, that's fine: I shall have succeeded in getting you going.

More people than I can remember have helped me write this: all my teachers, for a start, and my tutors (not least C. S. Lewis); then, my colleagues, and all the pupils who have ever written essays for me. I'm glad to acknowledge the help of Sophie Goldsworthy with the initial planning of the book, and the contributions of those who troubled to read chapters in draft and explain some of the blunders: Christopher Busby, Anne Coldiron, Paul Cheshire, Robert Cummings, Neville Davies, David vander Meulen, my son David S. Fowler, and the readers for the Press. Above all, I thank my wife, who put up with my preoccupation, as well as combing newspapers for good (bad) examples of how not to write.

A.F.

Edinburgh
2006

Contents

1. Pen and Computer

You can write only with your brain; but whether to process your thoughts with a computer or pen and paper is your first practical choice as a writer. I suppose it is still possible to ignore the computer and write just with pencil and paper. A surprising number of writers, including Martin Amis, A. S. Byatt, Ted Hughes, John Irving, Joyce Carol Oates, Susan Sontag, John Updike, and Edmund White prefer longhand for serious writing. But the advantages of the computer are so great that it seems almost irresponsible to pass them up. A computer greatly accelerates editing procedures, allowing you to take a piece through far more drafts than you could otherwise. On-screen correction is so easy that people of all ages find the process relaxing, even pleasurable. Computers give a sense of freedom from lasting error that no one who has experienced it will want to give up. I shall never forget the excitement I felt, twenty-five years ago, when I discovered that words had ceased to be indelible. So in this book I shall take for granted that you will probably use a computer for some, if not all, the processes of writing.

Many people use a computer throughout, and never feel the need to print out hard copy. Mathematicians, in particular, produce papers and even books entirely on-screen. In principle, it is possible to write and publish electronically, without ever lifting pen or pencil. For some, however, especially those engaged in literary work, this may not always be the way to get the most out of the computer.

Computers of the present generation have certain limitations, arising from the screen display, which for some people tend to complicate the process of writing long pieces. Even with the best flat-screen monitor you can't comfortably read long texts. And you can't actively browse with any clear sense of where you are in the text.

Good writing depends on extensive reading, not only previous reading of other works but also frequent scans of your own piece, the one you're working on. Yet if it runs to any considerable length, uninterrupted reading on-screen is difficult. A monitor's field of view is necessarily local, limited to about 150 words—much less than a printed page. This is fine for drafting a postcard; but not for extensive reading or browsing. To scroll through successive screenfuls is hardly an adequate substitute: it is too fragmentary and remote from ordinary reading. In active browsing you need to be able to skim or read a page or two here, check the index there, and jump back or forward at will, always aware of structure and proportion, always aware of each passage's relation to the text as a whole.

Working by the screenful can have the unfortunate consequence of smoothing your writing prematurely. For on-screen correction is so easy that the grammar and word choices gel too soon, without enough consideration being given to the overall sequence or the underlying structure. Decisions about the piece as a whole may tend to be passed over, so that the end result is polished enough, but boring: flat, shapeless, even garrulous.

Some have gone so far as to argue that the fluency and facility of composing on-screen are positively bad for writing, since they make you forget the reader's experience of your piece. The beautiful screen is supposed to delude us into a false consciousness, flattering us with the illusion that technical procedures (correction of typos, format changes, boilerplate insertions, rearrangement of phrases, and the like) can do it all by magic. You cast wonderful spells, but find they are somehow not enough. But the evidence for all this (cited by Edward Mendelson in a 1990 *Academic Computing* article) is no longer thought compelling. In any case, the remedy is a very simple one: any limitation you feel in the computer's display can be overcome by printing out hard copy. I shall assume, in fact, that you will work from printouts whenever you find it more convenient to do so.

Composing on-screen, revising as you go, is obviously fine for short letters, emails, and routine reports. But many people find that anything longer than 250 words or so—and certainly any competitive or ambitious piece that needs much thought—is better printed out for reading and drafting. For many writers drafting is not a detour but the best way forward.

An additional reason for alternating screen and paper applies only to some writers, who find their thinking in front of a screen slower. After a time the computer has for them a dulling, even stupefying effect. Others report quite the reverse, finding that the computer's pleasurability encourages thinking on-screen, as Michael Heim claims in *Electric Language* (1987). People differ; but it does no harm to take a break from the screen every half hour or so, for your circulation's sake.

Some writers find it helps to jot down the earliest draft on paper, where they can vary the size of words for emphasis, use abbreviations, and resort to private symbols. Even illegible scribbles can be turned to account: paper writers can postpone resolution of ambiguities, defer grammatical structuring, delay lexical choices, allow their minds to explore vague surrounding associations, and perhaps encounter serendipities. For them, the computer closes off too many syntactic options, and calls for definition of ideas still inchoate. Other writers, however, more at ease on the keyboard, value the rapid rearrangement and deletion that can be done on-screen. Inserts can go in as they come to mind, without need for memos or post-its. In drafting, the choice between pen and keyboard may be partly a matter of age, partly of training and temperament.

At any rate, when you have reached the stage of a rough OUTLINE, you may want to print it out for ease of reading. Working with the draft on paper, you can read it more easily, and see whether each passage is proportioned and positioned where it should be. But don't forget to have the latest draft on-screen, ready for you to slot in corrections, references, and new ideas.

Except for a complete beginner, computer spellchecks can waste time. They have a way of giving the correct spelling of the wrong word. Better to have a good dictionary on disk (or on your desk), and consult it for yourself. When you work on the final draft, though, a spellcheck sometimes finds inconsistencies. A grammar check, too, if it is a very good one, can be instructive. But again it is better still to learn some grammar. If you could have a program to write the whole piece for you without effort on your part, would you buy it? If the answer is yes, read no further.

2. Material Reading

To write, you need first to read; 'writing is an offshoot of reading', says Anita Brookner. Or writing can be thought of as conversation with people who are absent: when your turn to speak comes, it helps to remind yourself of what they have said. Besides, 'it's always easier to draw from the storehouse of memory than to think up something original' (Montaigne). To have ideas and words in memory, however, you must at some time have read or heard them. In a sense everything you have ever read provides the thought and vocabulary of your own writing. More immediately, though, you can read to gather the materials you need for your new piece.

Purposeful reading calls for an appropriate speed. Some think of reading as a passive state in which words scroll past at a rate fixed by nature, by the fact that you are a 'fast' reader or a 'slow' one. But anyone can learn to read at different speeds, and select the one that suits the task. Fast reading, slow reading, skimming, local analysis: each has its advantages and limitations. Fast reading leaves a more distinct impression of argument and structure but misses subtleties. Slow reading registers the fine grain of figures and textures, but sometimes in focusing on trees misses the wood. Skimming (glancing through cursorily) rapidly gathers instances or main points of an argument; it forms a broad impression and sometimes a false one. Browsing (idly dipping at random) searches unsystematically for matters of interest or to gain an impression of quality. It is best done off-screen: 'browsing' in computer terminology refers to a different, more directed activity.

Always combine goal-oriented reading with note-taking. In fact, it's a good idea to try to annotate most of what you read seriously, even when you have no special purpose. Annotation forms your views and helps you find your way around the text later (perhaps much later); it strengthens your memory. But aim to keep the annotation brief: very short phrases are enough to sum up the content, note topics of interest, points to look up, arguments to question, things to remember. If the text develops an argument, make a brief abstract of it. How brief is brief? To begin with, your notes may be depressingly long—longer than the text itself, perhaps. Later, when you recognize commonplaces, your notes can be more succinct—perhaps only a phrase per page. Compressing and expressing in your own words is an effort, but an effort worth making. It helps you to come to terms with the ideas and perhaps assimilate them.

The notes can go on index cards or in a notebook, or can deface the margins of a disposable edition. Or you can entrust them to the computer, if you feel confident of being able to retrieve them years later.

Reading divides naturally into long-term and short-term projects. The œuvres of voluminous, canonical authors such as Malory, Wittgenstein, or Voltaire are not read in a day. Even if eventually you get round to reading every word of them, they clearly come in the category of long-term, back-burner projects. Such reading needs to be done at a speed the author requires; whatever time it takes, you surrender to the wonder and excitement of discovery.

Short-term reading to a deadline is a different sort of activity altogether. In such goal-oriented reading you yourself should be in command: you decide the pace, you pursue an objective of your own. Single-mindedly you gather the material your piece calls for—and nothing else. In the short time allotted, you may have to skim rather than read. There may be time only to confirm an impression, locate a quotation, detect a flaw in your adversary's position, or check that your own argument is supported as strongly as you thought. Occasionally you may gut a whole book for a single fact, without compunction. Or you may reread a page of Martin Amis, just to verify you have been just in calling him repetitious. In skimming a work for its main gist, you may concentrate on the structure of sections and subsections, focusing perhaps on paragraph topics. (See Chapter 6.)

Annotating short-term reading is a hasty, scrappy business, for the material gleaned may be no more than a few scribbled phrases on scraps of paper, to be used or discarded within minutes. If there are long quotations, you can save time by photocopying or scanning them, then numbering and cuing them for insertion later. Shorter passages can be signalized by underlining, highlighting, or numbered references cued in your notes. If you use index cards, a sorting tray may be useful; but for a few slips of paper foldback clips are enough. In all this, don't forget that excessive organization easily substitutes for thought.

If you plan to write much—certainly if you mean to write history or literary criticism or cultural studies—you will need a programme of reading. Comparisons, in particular, call for a wide range of knowledge. Acquiring this will take time: you are not going to become well read by five o'clock tomorrow. But from the start you can taste books for yourself, rather than depend on the judgements of others. Moreover, you don't have to read every word of every author: sampling, dipping, skimming, and browsing are all quite legitimate. Above all, read what you enjoy— and read it omnivorously, with your eyes hanging out. The secret of becoming well read is not to let yourself be bored for long. So never force yourself on and on, struggling against a deep-seated disinclination. When boredom threatens, it may well be best to switch to another reading project. The well-read poet and botanist and anthologist Geoffrey Grigson would keep half a dozen books on the go at once; and some good scholars have diversified even more than that. Multifarious reading helps to develop a sense of literature's proportions: a sort of 'perfect pitch'.

Some great books seem quite impossible to get through. In such cases, try prescribing yourself a page or two per day, or just a paragraph. As you get on the author's wavelength you may gradually gain confidence, and almost begin to enjoy the book. Then, an appetite may grow: a thirst to devour not only that one book but the author's whole œuvre—and then to explore every major author in the traditional canon, in Harold Bloom's canon, or in one of your own discovery. And then you may want to taste the minor authors too. As a young man I couldn't read Henry James at all; now, though, he is a favourite author. Until you get to know the canon, a good idea is to read rather more literature than criticism.

Each stint of composition should begin with something easy, like reading a few paragraphs of a good essayist, to put you in the mood. 'Reading is to the mind what exercise is to the body' (Richard Steele). Then move on to material you have already annotated. This has the double advantage that it convinces you of the possibility of writing, and sets benchmarks for it. Finally, review your notes, select, and begin.

3. Beginning

A very few gifted individuals can write in one go (or say they can): they are able to sit before a blank page or screen, confidently expecting words to come, and find they do. But the rest of us, if we followed that method, would find the page still obstinately blank at the end of the writing session. For most sorts of writing, the best way to begin is not to. Or rather to have *already* begun in the past. If you make a big deal about the moment of beginning, it may never happen. Better avoid that heavy moment, then: read, think, annotate, work out the scale, do some outlining, scribble a few associations, and suddenly realize, 'How about that! I've started.'

Most people find that, rather than writing all in one go, it's better to take a piece through successive drafts. This means more work; but 'easy writing's vile hard reading', as the dramatist Sheridan said. Even the best writers go in for drafting: Kingsley Amis took *Lucky Jim* through ten complete drafts, and some of Dylan Thomas's poems went through as many as 300. The few writers who seem to have done little outward drafting (C. S. Lewis and Norman MacCaig, for example) have tended to possess the sort of memory that enabled them to draft inwardly. Ordinary writers had best think of two or three drafts at least, besides outlines.

Before you begin, there are preliminaries to think of

(see under PRACTICALITIES). Some writers like to warm up by reading for pleasure, some by doing word exercises. In the long term, exercises can have a useful training effect: they add to your repertoire of writing options. But when you're actually making a start they easily distract from the specific piece you have in mind. Besides, limbering-up exercises may turn attention to word selection too soon, and so get in the way of later DRAFTS.

The writing you invent will largely derive from previous reading and thinking, some of it imperfectly remembered. So it makes sense to refresh your memory with focused reading and skimming. If you have something like nine working hours before a deadline, you can spend, say, three hours reading and note-taking, informing yourself and reflecting on the issues. After all, you have to know enough to give substance to your opinions, however strongly you feel about them. Then another couple of hours might go on ordering your notes, looking up doubtful points, and clarifying your views. Theoretically that leaves four hours for writing. But in practice the phases are never entirely separate; they keep overlapping and interweaving in an organic way. In the midst of one procedure you get insights about another, perhaps, one you thought complete. That's fine: scribble a few sentences and set them aside for a later draft. It's best to attend to such inner promptings—to modify an opinion here, anticipate a later insertion there—before returning to the passage you are working on. Managing your time is not easy, though: you need to be firm with yourself, yet flexible.

As you mull over potential material in your notes, you

will begin to form a rough idea of possible topics for your piece. You will certainly know, for example, which passages that you read made most sense. From such reflections will come inklings of the thrust of what you mean to write. At this juncture you might give a moment's thought to probable readers and to how you want to affect them. But don't imagine the reader in any detail yet: the present aim is to find out what you want to say.

Now that you have a rough idea how many topics there are, you can work out matters of scale. This is an exciting stage, full of possibilities: you have complete freedom to put your ideas in order and arrange them in a provisional sequence.

You can begin, in fact, to do some rough outlining—and I really mean rough. A short piece on thatching for a local magazine, for example, might begin with jottings like these:

THATCHING (1,500 WORDS)

where used. Norfolk and?
construction
reeds vs heather vs turf
slates better?
insulation
how lasting?
fire regs
lost skill?
costly?
ornamental

If these are paragraph topics, the outline implies something like 2,000 words—too long for the proposed piece.

You might try compressing the outline by subordinating some of the heads:

materials
    slates vs thatch
    reeds heather turf

cost
    insulation
    special skills
    ornamental thatching
    durability

Once you settle on a feasible outline, you can start to slot in facts, references, and illustrative quotations. Under *cost*, for example, you might quote Belloc ('If I ever become a rich man ... I will build a house with deep thatch').

Outlining may seem easy, even mechanical—just a matter of counting sentences, topics, putting related items together, and assigning numbers to passages you intend to refer to or quote. All the same, the outline should not be rushed. Indeed, you may have to take it through several drafts, unless you use outlining software that facilitates instant rearrangement.

Whether you outline on-screen or on paper, it is a waste of time to agonize over grammatical decisions or tightly crafted phrases. At this stage private shorthand is better: jot down points from your notes, perhaps listing different opinions in drastically abbreviated form: 'A's fshnble theory; B's rbuttl' (A's fashionable theory; B's rebuttal). Such items may eventually be paragraph topics, so you need to work out what they imply as to scale. Without some idea of scale, indeed, no one can write anything. Imagine Melville beginning *Moby Dick*. If he hadn't planned a baggy monster of a book, he would not have known whether there would be room for an introductory Etymology, or for Extracts, or even for a tangential opening such as 'Call me Ishmael'.

Suppose you plan a 2,000-word report, implying about ten of your usual paragraphs. (Always think in terms of paragraphs.) If note-taking yielded twenty possible topics, you can simply select the more promising ten. But suppose your notes yielded only five topics? That's not a disaster; you simply allot two paragraphs to each of the five. Some people generally write more than is called for; others write less. If you belong to the first of these groups you may find it helps to play a trick on yourself by pretending the word-limit is lower—say 1,500. Then work towards the pretend figure, so that you don't produce superfluous words. If, on the other hand, you tend to write too little, pretend you have a more generous word-limit and can spread yourself as much as you like.

The next thing is to arrange the selected topics in a sequence that makes some sort of sense, although not necessarily in strict logical order. When you do this, leave plenty of room on the page between items for later insertions or reordering. You can now insert cues to quotations, to items from your notes, and the like. Label these by numbers or letters, keeping the actual material apart (on index cards or paper slips): at this stage you need to see the structural wood rather than the verbal trees. On-screen outlining is quicker: the quotations themselves can be keyed in straight away. If inserted materials are assigned a subsidiary level in the outline hierarchy, you can collapse them at will for a clear view of the structure. Alternatively, long quotations can be kept in temporary footnotes or separate files.

This first outline need not be *written*, in the ordinary sense. It can be set down in shorthand or even as a diagram. Use any abbreviations you like, or temporary memos: they don't even have to imply specific word choices. Brief phrases will pass. At this early stage fully grammatical sentences can be a positive drawback: settled grammar often gets in the way of redrafting. It is not malleable enough to be easily changed.

Say you are asked for a 500-word review of Bloggs's new textbook. Five hundred words might mean three longish or five shortish paragraphs. After reading the book and deciding what you think of it, you list possible topics:

1. B's previous work; his fitness to write on this new subject.
2. Survey of previous treatments; the state of current thinking; B's contribution.
3. Is B's book useful for beginners? How readable is it?

But what you actually put down needn't be anywhere near so intelligible as this to anyone else. Remember you are writing the outline for yourself alone. It might be enough to put something like this:

1. B's track rec[ord]
2. C's rev[iew] of D & E. B w[ith] it?
3. Primer? Gd read?

So now you have a draft. Everything in it is of course provisional; nevertheless the blank page is gone. Painlessly, you have made a start.

4. Drafts

Amateurs try to write in one go; professionals draft and draft again. Great exceptions come to mind, of course, like Joseph Conrad. Besides, pursuing a steady progress through drafts won't always exempt you from having to wrestle with the material. But in ordinary writing it should free you from being immobilized: being stuck in front of an empty screen or page. After all, you are not Conrad.

Drafting has been mentioned a few times; let's look at it now more closely. The first thing to know about drafting is the possible advantage of postponing so far as you can an exact choice of words. In your early drafts you may find it helpful to hold off from committing yourself to specific wording. Choice of words, which to the beginner seems the first step in writing, is more often actually the last. The way to effective writing is to defer word choice: certainly you should avoid letting your writing solidify too soon into elaborate grammatical structures that will hinder future revision.

What if you think of a great phrase? If you should be so lucky, of course put it in: your whole piece may well grow from the development of a few words you are sure of. But that can hardly be the basis of a general method. It may even be a good idea to write the lucky phrase down separately. On-screen it can be kept at a low outline level until you are ready for it. Brilliant wording should of course be used, but not necessarily looked for at this stage.

In drafts, wording needn't be final: you can use a provisional word, even if you suspect it probably won't, in the end, quite work. (You can add a memo to replace the word later; I use wavy underlining for this.) Private symbols are fine at this stage, even vague ones such as '→', which might mean 'becomes', or 'changes to', or 'develops into', or 'leads to', or 'causes'. Drafting should also be free from the seductive distractions of reference books and electronic databases. So avoid searching for references, spellings, quotations, or authoritative verdicts on minutiae of word usage. Instead, keep up the momentum: the business in hand is merely to arrive at a provisional, more or less continuous draft—a sequence of ideas you can subscribe to.

The earliest draft, as we saw, is merely a selection from your reading and notes: points that sketch out your position, or perhaps points you have still to decide about. A bare list of points is enough, if possible in a sensible sequence. You need only represent each item by a word or phrase, possibly with a cue to material stored elsewhere; a good plan is to arrange the phrases in a column. Already the draft shows how many topics you are writing about, and so whether you're roughly in scale. You may also be able to guess from the sequence what the shape of an argument or exposition may turn out to be. Reach out to it in imagination: is it mostly description, or narrative? You might try to decide, tentatively, what kind of piece you have embarked on.

Before taking the draft further, check for relevance each item listed: is it directly relevant to your viewpoint, or only peripheral? Think, too, how you will get it across: which points are self-evident enough to be merely stated and exemplified, and which are going to call for extensive support.

Next rearrange the projected items to form a coherent sequence (this is easy on-screen; on paper it may require a new draft). Quickly reviewing each item in turn, ask yourself, How am I going to get from A to B in this paragraph? How many sentences is it likely to take? The answer may show that the draft contains too many items or—much less likely—too few. You can easily adjust this right away, altering the number of topics to be treated in full. (The other topics will be mentioned briefly or deleted altogether.) Allow for long quotations in your estimate, and check you are still in scale; never let the word count run away from you.

If the piece is to have a connected argument, you may find it not too soon to put down a few connectives and conjunctions (but, because, since, although, and the like) to articulate the sequence of thought. Later, these will assist your choice of PARAGRAPH TYPES. Suppose your draft begins:

A's arg[ument]
but B's!
B's position undermined by new evidence
Evid[ence] sound?

Here, you might think of planning a two-part paragraph:

(1) new evidence against B
(2) its shakiness counts in A's favour.

So the first draft is arrived at by browsing through your notes (a thing easier to do on paper) and jotting down topics—more of them than you will need—in case some don't work out. The topics may be no more than a bare list of phrases. You needn't go into the train of thought in detail, unless as a memo; and, if you plan to quote and discuss a passage, list it but leave the discussion itself until later.

The next step is to flesh out this skeleton with more detail, adding examples and arguments in support or opposition; and inserting quotations and phrases gathered earlier. Your own words, however, can be left in summary, even abbreviated form: 'ex[ample] from Smith, ref[erence] from Jones; X's arg[ument] ag[ain]st Y'. This is more or less the method used by a journalist in Michael Frayn's novel *Towards the End of the Morning* (1967): 'T prob of t multi-racial soc is in ess merely t mod versn of t time-hon prob of unitg tribes in nationhd'. Others use *t* for 'to'; *th* for 'the'; *wh* for 'who' or 'which'; and so on. But beware: the more drastic the abbreviations, the sooner they become unintelligible. You may find it works better to have less abbreviation but also less grammar: 'multi-racial soc. prob. same as old prob of tribes & nation'.

Now you are ready for a continuous draft. So far you have used indicators of content: abbreviations, incomplete sentences, private symbols. Now you can spell these out in full, although of course the words you write may not all figure in the final draft. This first continuous draft should be a spontaneous expression; forget about problems of grammar, forget correct spellings (for the moment!), forget searching for the precise word, and forget finely polished phrases. Concentrate on the flow of ideas and words, expressed in the simplest possible way. It is a good idea to keep the word order to SVO (subject verb object): 'The man bit the dog' is better, at this stage, than 'the dog was bitten by the man'. This is because the more flexible SVO order keeps your options open for later reshaping. Shape first, polish after.

The continuous draft should be written as fast as you can, if possible in one unbroken stint. Many writers discover fluency through the action of writing—perhaps after a longish spell of writing, at that. So give yourself a chance: ready inspiration may strike only after an hour or so. If you are a costive writer, it may help to try a few minutes of automatic writing (that is, uncensored, uncontrolled, spontaneous scribbling of whatever comes to mind: free association, however 'incorrect' or nonsensical). If nothing else, automatic writing will prove you can be fluent when you don't try.

For the sake of momentum, keep to a writing mode as much as possible: forget readers for the time being. Once you get going, race ahead and give yourself free rein; don't stop to consult databases or books. But try to be conscious of the unfolding sequence of thought, and keep marking it with words like 'but', and 'nevertheless', and 'for example'.

Next print out this connected draft, numbering the pages so as to be able to find your way around it. Read it with an eye to internal relevance—continuity of thought, consistency of argument—and mark any cuts or additions called for. Yet again, check for scale: estimating your usual average sentence length can give you some idea of the word-count implied by the paragraphs you planned. A long paragraph of twenty sentences will need to be balanced against a short one; inserting a long quotation can soon turn a short paragraph into a long one. By now, some of your paragraphs should be starting to have shape and size. If they seem too long, be ruthless in REDUCING them. It doesn't pay to get attached to the words of an early draft; as always, your best friend is the wastepaper basket.

In later drafts you can introduce more detail, fix the paragraph topics and paragraph types, work out arguments step by step, and settle on locations for material from your notes. Leave a draft aside as long as possible before carrying it further: that gives you a chance to mull over the piece unconsciously. Besides, after a lapse of time errors and inconsistencies come to stand out more conspicuously.

You can now begin revising from the specific viewpoint of READERS. Once you know what you have to say, it's time to think about explaining it to others. Imagine people reading your piece, and work at making it utterly clear to them. At each point you need to be sure you are not assuming knowledge of a later passage: in this sense there should be a single linear sequence throughout your piece. Be certain to close off every ambiguity, even if it is only a momentary one.

When you feel ready, do a draft with the aim of smoothing out the flow. You can allow yourself now a few inverted or passive sentences (OVS, or object–verb–subject) where these can help: 'when you yourself know what you want to say, it is explained easily to others'. At the same time, make any local changes that suggest themselves for the sake of clarity, cogency, momentum, and variety. Get rid of obscurities, awkwardnesses, overloading, and repetitions. If you can, show this draft to a friend: you may get useful feedback, perhaps prompting enough changes to suggest a whole new draft. That wouldn't be a setback, since it would take you nearer your readers.

Previously, considerations of words and grammar were postponed. But in later drafts you will be framing SEN-TENCES and thinking of large-scale features such as PERFORMANCE AND CONCURRENCE.

5. Outlines

Outlining has already been touched on; but it is so indispensable that we need to look at it more fully. Every longish piece of writing is the better for an outline setting out the overall plan. Outlines have two main aims: to control the number of parts (and consequently the scale) and to determine the sequence of parts. Considerations of scale affect writing at every point. If quotation seems called for and your word limit is 300, it would be futile to think of quoting more than a phrase or two. Or suppose you are asked for a bio (biographical statement) of fifty words: effectively that implies three or four sentences, on, say, your education, work experience, and publications. It is unprofessional to put finger to keyboard or pen to paper without any idea of the scale of a piece; no one has time to write words that will have to be discarded. However repugnant it may be, then, you will have to get used to working out the scale at every stage. First, quantify the outline in paragraph units. A ten-page, double-spaced essay implies about 2,500 words, about fifteen screenfuls, or roughly ten paragraphs of 250 words each. An average short paragraph is likely to comprise five to ten sentences of 20 to 30 words each; a long paragraph might be double that, or more. So, you are looking to write ten medium-length paragraphs.

Scale also determines how much of the time available

should be given to reading or research, to note-taking, to gathering material from your notes, to thinking, to outlining, and (finally) to writing. Some writers become alarmed at how much time they are spending on a mere outline. They naturally feel impatient to make a start on 'real writing', 'writing itself'. But time spent on the outline is seldom wasted. It clarifies trains and proportions of thought that would otherwise remain vague or confused. Working out a sequence of parts is vital, for no one can write without at least a rough idea of what is to come next. Moreover, outlining enables you to keep in proportion, so that even if you find yourself running over the word limit you will be able to adjust some of the topics without losing all the work already done.

From the working outline you can easily produce a formal outline or abstract, if you need one for an editor or instructor. The abstract, being meant for another reader, should be grammatical, and may have to follow an instructor's special requirements (that it should be expressed in complete sentences; that it should be expressed in incomplete sentences; etc.). By contrast your working outline is for your eyes only, and can be as rough as you like. You may use private symbols in it, shorthand, or abbreviations (see DRAFTS).

To begin an outline, browse through your notes and jot down promising topics; some people find this more difficult on-screen. Select more topics than you expect to treat, in case some don't work out. To represent the topics, single words or fragmentary phrases will do. Waste no time forming grammatical structures: they are unlikely to survive in future drafts. All the same, the outline should fairly indicate the subjects you are mooting. It needn't be a logical analysis: at this stage the heads don't even have to be of the same importance or generality. It's enough if each head represents an idea that will need treatment at something like paragraph length. The *number* of headings, however, should be more tightly controlled, since it tends to fix the length of your piece. Some writers even like to begin with paragraph numbers and add contents, as if completing a form.

Next, you arrange the heads in a coherent order. One way of doing this is to use a linear *sequence*; another is to draw a *web diagram*. The web (like a flow chart) locates the heads and key words in boxes joined up by lines or arrows showing their connections. In the sequence method, the heads follow one another in a single progression, perhaps with numbered or lettered subheads:

Report on planning the project
results of consultation
(a) with colleagues
(b) with advisers
general recommendation
quantification
wider implications
(a) departmental
(b) individual

Avoid elaborate systems of indentation and lettering; they easily become messy and confusing when you subsequently alter them. Marginal dashes are usually sufficient. This sequence method has the advantage of being readily converted to a series of paragraphs.

The web diagram is more useful for working out how the topics interrelate.

```
colleagues → results of consultation ← advisers
                        ↓
              general recommendation
                        ↓
  quantification → detailed recommendation
                        ↓
for department ← implications → for individuals
```

But any such diagram will have to be replaced at some stage by a single progression.

Next, start all over again, this time making the outline more detailed. Flesh it out, inserting phrases and quotations you have collected, references, and (inevitably) new points that have just occurred to you. If you mean to discuss particular passages in texts, indicate these, noting what you mean each discussion to show. But leave out the discussions themselves: there's no point in drafting what you may not have room for. It's enough at first to designate supporting arguments or examples quite summarily: 'exs & refs' (examples and references); 'X's arg agst Y' (X's argument against Y). For the arguments themselves and any quotations, reference numbers will do meanwhile: you can key or scan them in later. In a broad-brush outline details merely distract.

By now you should know how many paragraphs the topics are likely to require. So you can check whether the outline is feasible within the word-limit, whether the parts are in proportion, and whether each part is relevant to the subject—in short, whether the outline corresponds to your brief. If necessary, drop some of the heads. You will probably try to deceive yourself into keeping too many favourite topics; you may have to convince yourself by calculations based on paragraph size. Scale isn't all guess-work: long quotations, for example, can be quantified exactly. Besides, you can work out which points will need extensive supporting arguments, and which only need to be stated with examples. All this appraisal calls for determined honesty.

The outline can be set out logically, analytically, or in an argumentative way—or by any other method that works. A common sequence for a report goes

opening | narrative or analysis | argument | counter-argument | revised argument | conclusion.

When you come to the argument, ask yourself such questions as: How am I going to get from here to there convincingly? What are the points against me? At this stage, unless you deceive yourself, you are likely to find that new complications and unforeseen distinctions have emerged, which call for regrouping. Such rearrangement of headings is more easily done on-screen.

One advantage of having an outline is that you can write on individual parts whenever you like, without following a fixed sequence. You can develop any heading into fuller detail whenever you see your way forward with it. So it may be time to attempt a few paragraph outlines. Getting into the detail of a paragraph may well show you have given it too much to do: arguing a single point can take a surprising number of sentences. If this happens, check again for scale. If you have left yourself enough slack, you may be able to solve the problem by splitting the paragraph into two new ones. But if the probable word count is already pushing the limit, some of the heads will have to roll, or at least be reduced to mere passing mentions. Better lose a topic than run over the limit. Radical changes to your outline needn't cause you the slightest dismay; they are quite usual.

Working outlines are usually thrown away, so we must take a hypothetical case:

1. R's [Reeve's] election | 2. R's duties | 3. Examples of R as peasant leader against authority.

Suppose this was part of H. S. Bennett's outline for his chapter 'Manorial Administration' in *Life on the English Manor* (1938). As Bennett developed the third paragraph in more detail, he made the point that the reeve as representative of the peasants sometimes led them in resisting authority. Bennett had two examples of this: a case in which a Byland Abbey dyke was thrown down and a case in which pledged animals were rescued. The rescue example seems to have turned out so complicated as to need a long narrative. Nevertheless Bennett decided to give it in full, probably for its striking illustration of manners. One can imagine him accommodating it by adding an unscheduled paragraph:

1. R's election | 2. R's duties | 3. R as peasant leader agst authority | 4. Rescue case.

In the third paragraph here the two cases are briefly

considered; the whole of the fourth recounts the rescue of the animals.

A *formal outline* (as distinct from the working outline we have been looking at) need not concern us much: ground rules for it are generally laid down by the instructor—for example, as to whether it should be expressed in complete or incomplete sentences. The relation of heads to subheads, however, often causes difficulty. If you are working on paper, avoid a complex indentation system (heads full out, subheads progressively indented, etc.). Such a system easily becomes confused if the outline is modified; numbering or lettering the subheads allows more flexibility. On-screen, the problem hardly arises: an outline programme handles indentation systems easily.

Subheadings, whether numbered or not, must be plural. If there are only two subheadings, deleting one necessitates promoting the other to heading status. For a formal outline doesn't merely list topic heads: it is supposed to summarize the content, showing how each topic is handled and what conclusions are reached.

6. Paragraphs

The paragraph is a main unit of composition, as important to the writer as the sentence or the phrase. It develops a single topic, and so has a distinct, independent unity. As a distinct passage, it begins with a new line (often indented: the new line marks a break in sense from the previous paragraph, and consequently a breathing space). It may help to think of the paragraph as a box containing a bunch of closely related ideas about the topic. More dynamically, however, it is also a vehicle or programme that carries the sense on. At paragraph end your readers are in a different place from where they started; the paragraph has taken them from A to B. So it would not be a good plan to write your piece without divisions, as some do, and split it up into paragraphs later. Best write in paragraphs from the beginning.

One way to draft paragraphs is to repeat the list of points you drew from your notes, and put them into paragraph boxes, one topic apiece, together with related references, quotations, and other material (still in pre-grammatical shorthand). Check the scale of these 'paragraphs', on a rough basis of three to fifteen sentences each. If you are a profuse writer (that is, usually write more than is asked for), plan for the lower count of three sentences per paragraph. Once you have finished a detailed OUTLINE, you are ready to draft an individual paragraph.

In drafting a paragraph, you form a sequence of SENTENCES that together will make it work as a unit. To make a beginning, the paragraph takes a new breath, perhaps quite a deep breath. In general sentences follow on from their predecessors; but the first sentence of a paragraph needn't do so. It can begin a new topic altogether; in which case it may be a *topic sentence*, announcing what the paragraph is about. A topic sentence should be brief. Indeed, it can be extremely brief, especially in narrative; Jane Austen's *Pride and Prejudice* has a two-word topic sentence: 'They came.' Many writers use a rhetorical question to declare the new topic: 'And what of the British response?' But a sentence fragment can work just as well, leading on strongly, as in: 'Now for the response'. In expository writing, a topic sentence often refers back to an earlier passage, or forward to the next:

> We shall see in the next chapter how patterns, traditions, biases, cultural and other controlling assumptions have affected the writing of European and of American history in modern times.

> What validates any pattern, as we saw, is that it permits a meaning to be attached to otherwise dumb, disconnected facts.
>
> (Jacques Barzun, *The Modern Researcher*)

Good topic sentences can impart energy to a piece wonderfully.

Next, write something about this topic, perhaps giving the gist of your own view, or sketching the situation in a narrative sentence or two, or giving a reason for qualifying the initial statement. Then, restate in completely different words. (This rephrasing is important for clarity; besides, if no alternative words can be found to express an opinion, it may well be baseless, and have to be rethought.) Follow with sentences supporting your view: arguments, authorities, or illustrative examples. If the view is controversial you will have to acknowledge the potential objections, refuting each in turn. Try to do this fairly, without spin; you may learn something new, although perhaps only by losing the argument. Finally, taking all the discussion into account, restate your view again, but now necessarily in a modified form. Notice that your paragraph has taken you somewhere—from your initial view to a somewhat different one. Don't worry about inconsistency in this: you are allowed to think as you write. In fact doing so often makes the difference between a living paragraph and a dead one. A sentence of recapitulation may round off the paragraph, lead on to the next one, or simply give pause for thought. Before you leave the draft paragraph, see if you can summarize it briefly. If you can't, it will probably seem confusing to your reader too.

Here is a paragraph, labelled (within brackets) to show the various functional parts of the discourse:

> Looking back it now seems that our concept of ourselves as a nation and people reached a peak of naïve self-esteem in late Victorian times, a heady altitude from which we have been descending ever since. [TOPIC MARKER] We are not alone in this: other European countries have experienced similar changes of outlook. [QUALIFIER, BROADENING TOPIC] This

change has been accelerated by two world wars and by radical technological and political changes throughout the world; but a change of temper was apparent long before these developments. [EVALUATOR, *discounting external explanations*] Formerly, our attitude to the rest of the world was outward-looking. [ARGUMENT, *preferring internal explanation*] We annexed, administered, and developed large areas and sent missionaries to convert their peoples to our religion in the conviction that we were doing all this for their own good as well as ours. [DETAILED RESTATEMENT] Then gradually this tide turned. [TOPIC REVISED] We found it less easy to be quite sure that our way of life was necessarily the best. [RECAPITULATION: SUMMARIZER]   (G. M. Carstairs, *This Island Now*)

And here is another:

I turn to X. [TOPIC] X's views are dubious, yet his influence is considerable: a problematic situation. [VALUATION] His facts are often wrong: for example . . . [ARGUMENT 1] His inferences from them are weak. [ARGUMENT 2] His bad scholarship has repeatedly been unmasked, for example . . . [ARGUMENT 3] So the popularity of his writing must be based on extraneous factors. [CONCLUSION] It seems political analysis is called for. [REVISED VALUATION]

This is not the only sort of paragraph—nor the only way of analysing it; but it is a common pattern easily adapted to many uses.

Grammarians say the rules of grammar don't apply to

paragraphs, since these can have almost any size or shape. Certainly paragraphs are various in form, and have no rigid structure. But they can have a flexible programme or scenario, each component of which can be doubled or trebled, for example, if that serves the purpose. The common pattern discussed above is one such programme, and we shall look at others in the next chapter, on PARAGRAPH TYPES.

However firmly patterned a paragraph may be inwardly, it also needs to be flexible, even a bit unpredictable. Each of its sentences must contribute to the movement carrying the paragraph forward; but it needs to do so in a surprising fashion. It must avoid what James Thurber calls 'hardening of the paragraphs'. To this end you might try alternating lengths of sentences, as Twain does at the beginning of chapter 19 of *Huckleberry Finn*, in a paragraph understandably singled out by the American critic Harold Bloom for special praise:

> Two or three days and nights went by; I reckon I might say they swum by, they slid along so quiet and smooth and lovely. Here is the way we put in the time . . .

Keeping rhythms lively like this can make for buoyancy, or, when you want it, can put a driving impetus at your command. (Notice, too, Twain's simple lead-in to the narrative passage that follows.) Another master of paragraph rhythm is Walter de la Mare:

> It was just so inside. Everything was in its place. Not only the great solid pieces of substantial furniture which Mr. MacKnackery had purchased with his

> burlap money—wardrobes, coffers, presses, four-
> posters, chest-of-drawers, sideboards, tables, sofas,
> chairs—but even all the little things, bead-mats,
> footstools, candle-snuffers, boot-trees, ornaments,
> knick-knacks, Euphemia's silks and Tabitha's water-
> colours. There was a place for everything, and
> everything was in its place. Yes, and kept
> there.   (*Broomsticks*)

The short final sentence, apparently an afterthought, springs a little surprise in the rhythm and gets the paragraph to a crisp end.

As their writer, you will know your paragraphs' inner programmes; but you would do well to keep them hidden from readers. You may have worked hard, for example, to join each sentence to the one before by connections that make for continuity and give readers confidence to move forward. (As in mountaineering, you make sure of several secure holds before moving to a new one.) So, you might arrange links of similarity on a pattern such as *ab* | *bc* | *cd*:

> . . . grey walls . . .
> . . . walls and windows . . .
> . . . windows that open . . .

But any such method needs to be varied, to disguise what is going on. Suppose you wish to make a series of links with a previous paragraph. For the first link, you could take up an idea and restate it. For the next, take up only a word. For the next again, since the previous paragraph is now more remote, you might repeat a whole phrase, or make the connection explicit. Again, to disguise a sequence of examples you could stretch some to two or more sentences, while packing several others into one.

Always keep up momentum. The reader should never feel you are going on in the words and making no progress in the sense. Arranging items as a climactic sequence increases momentum, and so does changing the sentence length progressively. Similarly, repeating the same, simple grammatical construction tends to make for a rapid flow. And alternating between singulars and plurals can help to make clear what goes with what grammatically. In general, a clear sequence of items (logical, for example, or chronological), promotes easy uptake and a sense of movement from sentence to sentence. Ambiguities, on the contrary, impede flow:

> If I painted a picture on the side of your house, who would own it?

So make sure your pronouns have unambiguous antecedents. Before you end a paragraph, give a 'lead-in' preparing for the next.

Being self-contained, paragraphs can be written in any order. If one of them gives you grief, leave it alone and go on to the next, and so keep up your momentum. Gabriel García Márquez says how for him 'One of the most difficult things is the first paragraph. I have spent many months on a first paragraph, and once I get it, the rest just comes out very easily.' He claims that 'in the first paragraph you solve most of the problems with your book. The theme is defined, the style, the tone.' Admirable in a fiction writer, maybe, but a fatal example for ordinary writers. If the first paragraph proves difficult, don't on any account spend months on it, or even hours. Instead, go on without delay to the second or the third paragraph. Pascal's advice is good: 'The last thing one settles in writing a book is what one should put in first.'

Try to alternate short paragraphs and longish ones, of ten or even fifteen sentences. For this, *Treasure Island* is a useful model. The paragraphs in Robert Louis Stevenson's essays are less so: nowadays they often seem too long. But he knows how to vary them; in 'Walking Tours', for example, he follows a paragraph of two pages with one of three sentences. Some will dismiss attention to such matters as mere 'formalism'. But, like many other aesthetic configurations, it has a functional basis: the alternation of paragraph length gives a reader relief. By contrast, Stevenson's friend Henry James did not go in for alternating paragraph lengths, and that may partly explain why some readers find him difficult.

A very short paragraph, even perhaps a single isolated sentence, can arrest attention. But take care not to overuse this device: its effect would soon diminish. Moderately short paragraphs make for a fast read, and suit a journalistic treatment; but a series of many short paragraphs easily gives a breathless impression, or suggests you have not much to say.

Paragraphs being main units of writing, you may find it convenient to mull them over away from your desk. You can compose a paragraph while walking, as many good writers have done. In the days of audiotyping, it used to be possible to put together a paragraph on the way to work, speaking it into a tape notebook. But it is tedious transcribing from tape; generally it works better to commit the paragraph or short letter to memory.

In redrafting a paragraph, give particular attention to its unity. Ask yourself insistently, is this sentence closely relevant? Does it truly belong to the argument? In a descriptive paragraph you might ask, is this detail fully consistent with the others making up the account? Again, is the paragraph in the best place? Or should I rethink the sequence of paragraphs?

7. Paragraph Types

In practice, paragraphs take as many shapes as there are matters to communicate. So you may feel like going it alone and discovering for yourself, in each instance, which shape of paragraph your paragraph needs. On the other hand, you may find it helps to know in advance a few common patterns, if only to use them as points of departure.

In the last chapter I described an *argumentative paragraph* consisting of eight optional parts: topic, initial view, restatement, argument, objection, refutation, modified restatement, and recapitulation. Other common types are the *opening paragraph*; the *two-parter*; the *illustrative paragraph*; the *narrative*; the *expository paragraph*; the *enumerative paragraph*; the *quotation*; and the coda or *closing paragraph*.

The *illustrative paragraph*, a useful type, often comes right out with a broad assertion (a topic sentence in disguise) and continues with illustrative particulars. These particulars often form a series of staccato sentences:

> The British are either Sunday drivers or professional racing drivers disguised as reps. They drive too fast. They tailgate anyone presuming to impede them. They ignore pedestrians. They are contemptuous of stopping distances. And they have neither manners nor signals . . .

This pattern—generalization followed by particulars—can also be inverted: you can start with the examples and go on, inductively as it were, to form the general conclusion.

The *enumerative paragraph* is indispensable for description. Ruskin describes the Rhone river like this:

> Waves of clear sea are, indeed, lovely to watch, but they are always coming or gone, never in any taken shape to be seen for a second. But here was one mighty wave that was always itself, and every fluted swirl of it, constant as the wreathing of a shell. No wasting away of the fallen foam, no pause for gathering of power, no helpless ebb of discouraged recoil; but alike through bright day and lulling night, the ever-pausing plunge, and never-fading flash, and never-hushing whisper, and, while the sun was up, the ever-answering glow of unearthly aquamarine, ultramarine, violet-blue, gentian-blue, peacock-blue, river-of-paradise blue, glass of a painted window melted in the sun, and the witch of the Alps flinging the spun tresses of it for ever from her snow. (*Praeterita*)

The repeated structure of phrases ('ever-pausing plunge . . . never-fading flash . . . never-hushing whisper') evokes the Rhone's sameness ('always itself'), in contrast to the ever-changing sea. Yet enough of the river's various blues are listed to suggest its sameness is saved from monotony by an endless variety of colour.

Choose the *two-parter* if you want to set out opposite aspects or arguments, pro and con. It is a useful type for juxtaposing contrary points of view: positive and negative, optimist and pessimist, or diminishing and augmenting. It can develop either comparison or contrast, as in this paragraph about different sorts of length in fiction:

> There are two kinds of long novel. Long novels of the first kind are short novels that go on for a long time. Most long novels are this kind of long novel, particularly in America—where writers routinely devastate acres of woodland for their spy thrillers, space operas, family sagas, and so on. Long novels of the second kind, on the other hand, are long because they have to be, earning their amplitude by the complexity of the demands they make on writer and reader alike.   (Martin Amis, *The War against Cliché*)

Try for a back-and-forth motion between the things compared, so that readers don't have to remember all about the first thing when you go on to the second.

A comparison can also be presented as a pair of mini-narratives. Here is Nicholson Baker on ways the mind changes, in *The Size of Thoughts*:

> Occasionally a change of mind follows alternate routes. One belief, about which initially I would admit of no doubt, gradually came to seem more porous and intricate in its structure, but instead of moderating my opinion correspondingly, and conceding the justice of several objections, I simply lost interest in it, and now I nod absently if the topic comes up over lunch. Another time a cherished opinion weakened as I became too familiar with the three examples that advocates used over and over to support it. Under the glare of this

repetition, the secondary details, the richer underthrumming of the opinion, faded; I seemed to have held it once too often; I tried but failed to find the rhetorical or figurative twist that would revive it for me. I crept insensibly toward the opposing view.

In pro-and-con paragraphs it is worth considering seriously the opinion you don't yourself hold, entering into it as sympathetically as you can. This will make you seem even-handed and persuasive—and may help you to rebut the opposing view more effectively. To be an effective opponent you need to know your enemy's strength from the inside; Renaissance education (like Milton's at Cambridge University) used to include disputations or debates where the candidates didn't always know in advance which side they would have to defend.

In a *quotation paragraph*, the main item consists of a long quotation. Of course, the quotation is not quite the sole content: it needs to be applied to the purpose so that readers will understand exactly what it is there for (see under QUOTATION). After paragraphs of this type, a brief recapitulation may be needed, to return to the main line of the piece.

A *defining paragraph* clarifies what you mean by some key word or idea. You will probably use a dictionary definition for this; but don't quote it at any length unless you mean to improve on it (by updating, qualifying, or comparing it with another). The usual way to define a term is by treating it as a member of a larger class, and specifying what distinguishes it from others in the same class. So man is defined as an animal distinguished from others by being capable of reason (or laughter, or speech). This takes for granted the classes never change. To say man is distinguished by reason ignores the fact that some animals have proved to be capable of reason. To take historical change into account, a family resemblance approach acknowledging that shared features change over time may be helpful: describing a family of members can often make things clearer than the logic of sets. As Dr Johnson understood, describing something in specific detail sometimes conveys more than defining it in abstract generality—'Things may be made darker by definition.' Thus, a cow is defined as a horned animal; yet a particular cow may have no horns. Johnson's view is vindicated nowadays, when description relying on structures or associations tends to be preferred to definition based on categories.

For the coda or *concluding paragraph* you review the themes of the chapter as they have emerged from all the argument and qualification and detail; restating them in a reduced, simple form. Remember that some readers, browsing through your piece, will try to gather its gist from the chapter codas alone. As well as recapitulating, the coda often leads on, especially in a long piece, to topics of the section to follow.

The *recursive* or *loose paragraph* is possibly the commonest type of all. Its plan is to keep returning to restatements of the topic sentence, always adding some new aspect or additional argument. It is an untidy pattern, easier to write than to read. I have said it returns to the topic sentence; but what it returns to is more like a vague sense that a clearer topic is needed.

Another useful type of paragraph presents a list. Lists

are usually planned with a particular aim in mind. Take Charles Dickens's description of a junk-shop window—

> In front of the shop-window are ranged some half-dozen high-backed chairs, with spinal complaints and wasted legs; a corner-cupboard; two or three very dark mahongany tables, with flaps like mathematical problems; some pickle jars, some surgeons' ditto, with gilt labels and without stoppers; an unframed portrait of some lady who flourished about the beginning of the thirteenth century, by an artist who never flourished at all; an incalculable host of miscellanies of every description, including bottles and cabinets, rags and bones, fenders and street-door knockers, fire-irons, wearing apparel and bedding, a hall lamp, and a room-door.   (*Sketches by Boz*, ch. 21)

Here the master of listing suggests both the exhaustive-ness of an inventory ('ditto') and the indescribable miscel-laneousness ('incalculable host') that defeats it. Many rhetorical devices carry the reader along: repetition ('flourished ... flourished'), zeugma ('with ... labels ... without stoppers'), and defeated expectation, as when familiar pairings are followed by incongruities ('pickle jars' and 'surgeons'' jars of anatomical specimens).

Sometimes a list maximizes the quiddity or sheer thingness of the items, as in J. G. Farrell's evocation of an exhibition catalogue:

> Instrument to teach the blind to write. Model of an aerial machine and of a navigable balloon. A fire annihilator by R. Weare of Plumstead Common. A

domestic telegraph requiring only one bell for any number of rooms. An expanding pianoforte for yachts etc. Artificial teeth carved in hippopotamus ivory by Sinclair and Hockley of Soho. A universal drill for removing decay from teeth. A jaw-lever for keeping animals' mouths open. Improved double truss for hernia, invented by a labouring man . . .

(*The Siege of Krishnapoor*)

Here, patterning is less important than the extraordinariness of the items, which is further amplified by arbitrary specifics such as unusual proper names.

The *opening paragraph* comes last, as the most difficult—and because it is often best written last, after the others are secure. Its introductory remarks prepare readers for the piece to follow, giving a general idea of its topic and sometimes of its approach. In this paragraph type, exceptionally, it is usual for the writer to make a personal appearance. If you follow this convention, do so modestly. Explain simply how your approach is distinctive (*not* how it is better) and how it relates to other approaches. Claim nothing grand, for you have done nothing at all so far. Being on stage goes to some writers' heads, so that they indulge in ego trips, saying things like 'I wish to fully develop the representational problematic' or 'I want to begin by making it perfectly clear . . .' No one cares (at least at this stage) what the writer wants. Worse still, opening paragraphs easily degenerate into empty manoeuvring, abstract gesturing, or ideological manifestos, which can be seriously offputting to people who might otherwise have read the piece. So, on the whole, it may be best to plunge into the middle of what you have to say. In a news item, it is probably not a good idea to begin with irrelevant scene-setting—'On a torrid day last week, Jason was looking through his collection of first day covers . . .' Readers are impatient to know what your piece is about.

Another reason to write the opening paragraph last is that if the piece is worth anything you will only then know what it has achieved. When you eventually come to formulate the opening, you will probably wish to be succinct about your aims, knowing privately that they have not been accomplished. Self-deprecation is a good note for an opening paragraph. And it may be an idea to acknowledge who you are writing for: 'Readers may find it interesting to explore such-and-such . . .'

8. Arguments

It is easy to begin simply by asserting what you want to argue. But what then? Many continue with bald assertion after bald assertion; which is unlikely to convince people, unless they agree with you already.

The first thing to do in support of your assertion is to restate it in different words. Refreshing its verbal expression gives readers a chance to take up your meaning more exactly, from words that follow a different route or that may be more familiar to them. And you yourself will discover by restating whether the initial assertion can in fact be said in any other way. If it can't, it may be a house of cards, a merely verbal construct without substance. Through reformulating the assertion, in fact, you will get a better grip on its core idea. If then you become less certain, it may be time to try out the idea in conversation. Political leaders are said to try out whole speeches in private conversation like a man trying on ties in his bedroom.

After restating the assertion you may still want to argue for its truth or value. By 'argue' I don't mean construct syllogisms, although it does no harm to think out the logic of what you are saying—'We are all going to die; he is one of us; so he is not going to live for ever.' No, persuasion is usually what to aim for, rather than logical demonstration. You can persuade in many different ways, for example by strong instances: appealing to common experience or the historical record. Or by quoting the authority of respected authors. (These have to be chosen with care, with an eye to your probable READERS: no point in quoting sages to children, or Che Guevara to High Tories.) You can sometimes argue by confuting an opposite viewpoint; it may have weaknesses obvious from your own. Again, you can sometimes clarify words generally confused in discussing the issue in dispute. Finally, you may want to qualify your first assertion in the light of all that has been considered; indeed that will be fully expected of you in the recapitulation or summing up.

Another way to persuade is by developing your assertion more fully. Suppose you wish to make the point that good writing is more efficient than bad. First you state it: 'Good style is more efficient than bad.' Next you rephrase, replacing every substantial word in the first statement. This requires some expansion, since 'efficient' has several meanings: 'When you write something well, it is not only clearer and more pleasurable to read, but also more economical of effort.' Restating has clarified the ideas of efficiency and good style. And you could go on to unpack the initial assertion further, explaining that clear writing gives pleasure partly through rapid access of information. Or you might persuade by example, referring perhaps to the research project directed by E. D. Hirsch, which established beyond reasonable doubt that good style eases uptake of meaning. Again, you might look into possible objections to the assertion. Some object on principle to clear writing, since they believe (like the British poststructuralist Catherine Belsey) that 'suave, lucid style conceals ruptures and avoids the very words ideologically at issue'. Anticipating this objection you might write 'Elegance need not be evasive.' Or, more combatively, you could argue that some who dislike clear writing prefer difficult jargon because it obfuscates ideas that couldn't bear much examination. Alternatively, if you wanted a more moderate statement, you could say, 'So long as the rhetoric is honest, its elegance can only assist communication.'

Arguments and counter-arguments can often be combined, as in Macaulay's wordy attempt to rebut defence of Charles I on the ground that 'he had so many private virtues':

> We charge him with having broken his coronation oath; and we are told that he kept his marriage vow! We accuse him of having given up his people to the merciless inflictions of the most hot-headed and hard-hearted of prelates; and the defence is, that he took his little son on his knee and kissed him! We censure him for having violated the articles of the Petition of Right, after having, for good and valuable consideration, promised to observe them; and we are informed that he was accustomed to hear prayers at six o'clock in the morning! It is to such considerations as these, together with his Vandyke dress, his handsome face, and his peaked beard, that he owes, we verily believe, most of his popularity with the present generation.
>
> (Macaulay, 'Milton')

Here the repeated sentence structures, together with the vivid examples, are intended to overwhelm readers, despite the weakness of the argument. Logic is often less successful than indirect persuasion.

Macaulay's violent rhetoric of conviction is not of course the only way to persuade. For example, you may well prefer to maintain a more detached position not committing yourself outright. If so, you might keep in mind gentler formulas, suitable for polite disagreement:

Virtues, however, do not go quite to the mark . . .

There is some plausibility in this view; but . . .

It does not seem far-fetched to think that . . .

To put it a little differently . . .

You may sometimes need to offer a phrase tentatively, advancing and half withdrawing it again:

In a way

As it were

As might be said

So to say

As one might say

As if one were to say

If I might put it like that

If it is not nonsense to put it so extremely

But that may be to go too far.

Such qualifying phrases can help to suggest a neutral stance, implying perhaps how diplomatic you are. To some, however, such phrases will seem weak, craven, or disingenuous.

At all events, it would be a mistake to express strong

feelings without considering how readers are likely to receive them. If you say 'Robinson is a total bastard who should be hung, drawn, and quartered,' people may even feel 'I can't help thinking this Jones (or whatever your name is) may be a little bit biased.'

A chief point in argument is to assert only as much as can be substantiated. Better to understate, usually, than to exaggerate. Why say 'Everyone supported the Government,' when the evidence of a single dissentient voice will be enough to prove you wrong? It is surely better to put, instead, 'Many supported the Government.' Such considerations will decide how much you should commit yourself to claiming. But when you engage yourself in support of a strong position, try to give of your best by consistently amplifying the viewpoint: make sure all the modifiers and qualifiers tend the same way, and attend to any unsupported assertions.

You will not convince readers if you use language that obviously depends on dogmas of an ideological system. Whether the system is Christian, atheist, or agnostic (or Marxist, Buddhist, nihilist, or deconstructionist) makes no difference to this. Jargon or formulaic language will suggest you are not troubling to rethink the matter; which your readers may take as a sort of insult.

Thinking afresh (or seeming to) is a strong point of the writings of Richard Rorty, the American philosopher. If you wish to persuade, it is worth studying Rorty's oblique method, as he considers the case for dualism, for example, in *Philosophy and the Mirror of Nature*. The question is whether 'sensation' and 'brain process' are just two ways of talking about the same thing.

The question now arises: Two ways of talking about *what*? Something mental or something physical? But here, I think, we have to resist our natural metaphysical urge, and *not* reply 'A third thing, of which both mentality and physicality are aspects'.

Why not (one might ask)? Why not propose this third thing? Here Rorty, seeming to share his reader's temptation to an easy metaphysical solution ('we have to resist our natural urge'), in effect rules out what would be a difficult objection for him to refute. He does this by suggesting that to make the objection would be to succumb to what is no more than a 'natural metaphysical urge'. Now Rorty anticipates a further objection, by pretending to propose a strategy against himself:

> It would be better at this point to abandon argument and fall back on sarcasm, asking rhetorical questions like 'What is this mental–physical contrast anyway? Whoever said that anything one mentioned had to fall into one or other of two (or half-a-dozen) ontological realms?'

This would actually be a fair point, but Rorty calls it 'disingenuous', since it is 'obvious' that ' "the physical" has somehow triumphed'. Left at that, one might resist his assumption that the physical is all there is. But Rorty goes on to face the difficulty more directly:

> But what did it [the physical] triumph over? The mental? What was that? The practice of making incorrigible reports about certain of one's states? That seems too small a thing to count as an intellectual

revolution. Perhaps, then, it triumphed over the sentimental intellectual's conviction that there was a private inner realm into which publicity, 'scientific method' and society could not penetrate. But this is not right either.

Apparently taking the reader into collaboration Rorty deflects an awkward point by pretending to hold it, then withdrawing from it as untenable, while making this defeat less unpalatable by minimizing the victory of materialism ('too small a thing').

This subtle, oblique form of persuasion should not be imitated without caution; it easily descends into slippery and unsound rhetoric. But there are tactics to be learned from Rorty. While you should not sail under false colours, you needn't, either, wave your flag in the reader's face.

9. Signposts

In a piece of any great length—say, over a thousand words—readers may need to be guided through the longer paragraphs, through the more complicated paths of argument or exposition. In short, they may need *signposts*. These signs or directional markers signal where to withdraw attention from one topic and view the larger picture, or where to turn to the next topic. Or they may indicate how two passages connect.

Signposts are sometimes explicit statements about what you have done, what you plan to do, what digressive side-trip you propose, or what you hope to achieve. But such explicit announcements, however practical, seem very writer-centred, so that readers often find them a serious turn-off:

> My need to exploit both inward- and outward-facing aspects of the tool grows from my study . . . My contribution will be to try to answer two questions . . .

> In this chapter I take the occasion of such-and-such for two distinct sets of reflections. In the first place . . .

Explicit signposts work better if kept brief and impersonal:

> So much for A. B was made of sterner stuff.
> To go into a little more detail, take the case of C.

Be especially wary of signposts promising great things in the future. You may not be able to avoid telling your readers 'I shall discuss such-and-such later.' But they may want to hear about such-and-such now, and they distrust signposts making promises such as 'I shall rebut So-and-so's entire argument in the next chapter.' Signposts can only point to the road, not go along it.

The most economical and least ambiguous signposts are often those that simply enumerate. A statement of intent followed by letters, numbers, or number words plainly signals a succession of implementations: '(a); 1.; First; Secondly; In the second place . . .' Much street furniture of this sort, however, can have a chilling effect. This especially applies to *analytic numbering* such as 4. 4. 4, meaning 'chapter 4, section 4, paragraph 4'. Such numbering is much used in scientific contexts, in linguistics, and in the lecture room. It can be valuable for its economy and precision; but some readers (and not only the innumerate) are easily put to flight by an invasion of numbers.

Introducing a larger section calls for something more elaborate in the way of signage:

In the previous chapter I argued such-and-such. Now we have to consider why a necessary consequence of this is . . .

I shall try to make this claim more precise.

This point calls for fuller treatment at chapter length.

To historicize Y is . . . to open up a new perspective . . . a perspective from which the remainder of this book will be written . . .

This is clear enough, but may strike some as too explicit. In such cases, dryness threatens, so that it is worth introducing a figurative expression:

> This point challenges careful exploration.
>
> Here we need to look at the small print.
>
> Let us now zoom in on some of the details.

The figures used for this purpose will have to be fairly obvious, of course—in fact, already losing their interest as metaphors—if they are not to distract the reader.

Signposts often work best (paradoxically) when they are implicit or disguised. It may be enough to repeat a phrase or keyword in the next topic sentence. Or, beginning a new paragraph with *But* may announce obviously enough that a contrasting view comes next, or at least a distinct aspect. Signposts can have a low profile and still be conspicuous enough. For example, after analysing a topic into several aspects—

> Modernizing for its own sake is a useless exercise, institutionally, technologically, and educationally.

—you might repeat the same words in the topic sentences of a subsequent expansion, or in similarly prominent positions:

> Technologically, new methods may be less effective than the old. Educationally, modernizing without adequate cohort studies often lowers standards. Institutionally, modernizing may well shake things up; but in doing so it loosens chains of command, and distracts from the pursuit of efficiency.

Signposts can be disguised by combining them with other elements such as topic sentences (as in the previous example). Structures on a large scale, like paragraphs, can be signposted by logical connectives: 'but; and; consequently; on the other hand; on the contrary; despite all this'. Usually, however, these connectives are supported by other sorts of signposts: by themselves they are clear but dull. See under PERFORMANCE AND CONCURRENCE.

Sentences within a paragraph, or whole paragraphs, can be juxtaposed without any connective other than indentation or the full-stop-and-space between sentences. This may be the best way in a report, for example, where space is at a premium. Otherwise, it helps your readers if you carry them forward with a transitional word or phrase. The transition may often be a mere aside without strong grammatical links backwards or forwards. Yet it can usefully change the tone or signal a new direction. So it resembles a signpost, and may be combined with it.

Here are some transitional formulas for linking paragraphs:

And
But
To turn to a closely related matter
To come to particulars
The last point needs further explanation
To go further in the same direction
To amplify this a little
But to return
To resume (*after a digression*).

One of the simplest transitions is a question, asked at the

end of one paragraph and answered in the next topic sentence:

But why did they build with brick rather than stone?
The answer is plain: mason's work was far more costly.

Similarly, you can start a paragraph with a sentence summarizing the previous one:

If the difficulties of building in brick were many and complicated, those of freestone were fewer but harder to overcome, often coming down to one: expense.

Inside a paragraph, the argument can be signposted economically by simple repetition or succession. But additional markers sometimes make the path more obvious. Useful transitions include: at the same time; presently; meanwhile; in consequence; consequently; so; but; nevertheless; even so; on the other hand; on the contrary; however; still; nonetheless; therefore; indeed; in fact; thus; yet; although; moreover; in sum (repeating and summarizing); in brief; in a word; what I want to insist on here is; etc. Despite what grammarians used to say, *But* and *And* can both be used to begin a sentence. Frequent use of *and* makes for a rapid, fluent pace; not so with *but*, repeated use of which easily becomes confusing.

To introduce an example or quotation, you have a large repertory of phrases to draw on: for example; for instance; or another example; to exemplify; to illustrate; to give an obvious instance; it is in X that Y can most clearly be observed; in the following more unusual example we find;

perhaps the best example that could be chosen is; such as the following; etc. Or you may prefer to content yourself with a simple colon (see under QUOTATION).

10. Sentences

Parts of sentences used to be classified elaborately; and it still helps to know how to take sentence structures apart. But detailed grammatical analysis needn't be a main concern in writing. If you should happen to dislike grammar for some reason, you can make do well enough with a survival kit of basic information about sentences and their parts.

A *sentence*, the unit of independent meaning, normally includes a subject and a verb, and may also have an object, or a complement, or both:

The cat vanished. [The cat *subject*, vanished *verb*]

The cat found the bird. [The cat *subject*, found *verb*, the bird *object*]

The cat found the bird satisfying. [The cat *subject*, found *verb*, the bird *object*, satisfying *complement*]

Such sentences consist of a single *clause* (a clause being a word group usually larger than a phrase), and they have a single subject–verb connection. Less simple sentences may consist of multiple clauses and verbs:

The cat found the bird satisfying, although he preferred mice.

A sentence may also contain *phrases*, that is, word groups without the subject–predicate structure: verb phrases;

adverbial phrases; adjectival phrases; pronoun phrases; or (the commonest type) noun phrases. A noun phrase can be the *subject, object,* or *complement* of a clause:

> She had read with avidity. [with avidity *adverbial phrase*]

> Her unexpected survival baffled me. [Her unexpected survival *noun phrase, subject*]

> She had read the books. [the books *noun phrase, object*]

> She had read almost all the many interesting theoretical books in the library. [almost . . . library *noun phrase, object*]

As can be seen, the noun phrase is an extremely flexible, productive construction.

Sentences and sentence fragments can function as statements, commands, exclamations, or questions (straight or rhetorical). Or they can simply be echoes: 'What rain!' 'Rain nothing: it's a downpour.' No fixed boundaries separate these types: one of them is easily transformed into another merely by changing the tone: 'The cat walked. The cat *walked*!'

Clauses, whether *main* (independent) or *subordinate*, all have the same seven structural patterns:

SV The cat pounced [The cat *subject*, pounced *verb*]

SVO The cat found mice [mice *object*]

SVC The cat felt hungry [hungry, what the cat was, is the *complement*]

SVA The cat went along the wall [along the wall *adverbial phrase*]

SVOO	The cat gave the magpie a fright [a fright *object*, the magpie *indirect object*]
SVOA	The magpie pecked the cat on the neck [the cat *object*, on the neck *adverbial phrase*]
SVOC	The magpie made the cat hopping mad [the cat *object*, hopping mad *complement*: the cat *was* hopping mad]

(where S = subject, V = verb, O = object, C = complement, and A = adverbial phrase).

Such analyses may seem to do no more than attach labels; but once identifying the functions is habitual, many useful transformations become easier. One of the most useful is changing passive to active (or vice versa). In this transformation the subject of the passive sentence moves to the end to become the object of an active sentence:

He was impressed by Andre Agassi.
→ Andre Agassi impressed him.

Here the passive agent (*He*) becomes the object of the new sentence (*him*), while the passive verb (*was impressed*) becomes active. Since passive constructions use more words, replacing them by active constructions is economical. But economy is not the only consideration: a commoner reason for making this transformation is to avoid ambiguity:

Agassi impressed him. He knew image was not everything.

The pronoun *He* is ambiguous: it might refer either to *Agassi* or to the person *impressed*. Changing to the passive is an easy way to avoid the ambiguity:

He was impressed by Agassi, who knew image was not everything.

This transformation is so often called for that it soon becomes more or less automatic.

Several main clauses can be combined to form longer sentences, either *compound* or *complex*. In compound sentences the main clauses are often joined by a conjunction (*and, or, but, as*, etc.):

She put the cat out and locked the door.

He sensed the old affliction had returned to haunt him, as it had before on this anniversary.

Alternatively the main clauses of the compound sentence can be juxtaposed without any joining word. This calls for heavy punctuation, semicolon or colon; avoid a comma link unless the two clauses are very closely connected, as in rapid narrative:

She fired once, the burglar went down.

If the connection between the main clauses is not immediately obvious, better use a conjunction. That is sometimes indispensable, as in

She had no dress sense; she wore fashionable clothes.

Here some conjunction is needed, to specify how the clauses are related and so clarify the sense. For example:

She had no dress sense, yet she wore fashionable clothes.

Or, with slightly different emphasis,

> She wore fashionable clothes, but she had no dress
> sense.

The US critic Mark Krupnick fancifully writes of a 'para-tactic syntax [one without conjunctions] that is American and democratic in refusing to reduce any phrase to relative status'. It would be better to think of paratactic construc-tions as helping the flow; for *which*-clauses sometimes tend to sound stiff.

So much for compound sentences. *Complex sentences* have at least one clause (called *subordinate*) that depends on another, the *main clause*:

> She wore fashionable clothes because they made her
> attractive to other women.

Here, the main clause 'She wore fashionable clothes' could stand on its own, whereas the subordinate clause 'because ... women' could not. Complex sentences rely more on grammatical structure, and so are able to convey subtler shades of meaning. In the example, much turns on *because*. A continuation might select one latent meaning or another: 'because, she thought, they made her more attractive'; 'because she *thought* they made her more attractive'; 'because, of course ...'; 'purely because ...'; 'she thought, wrongly ...'; 'ostensibly because ...'. Such nuances are less easily available with simpler structures like 'She wore fashionable clothes; they made her more attractive.'

In writing a complex sentence, be sure to put the main idea in the main clause; otherwise you may go badly wrong. Complex sentences are often mishandled by loading too much information into the subordinate clauses, which should be kept brief:

> When she bought clothes she used always to choose the most fashionable rather than those in a classic style.

The subordinate clause 'When she bought clothes' is as brief as could be. Contrast

> When she was buying clothes and both currently fashionable and classic styles were available, she always chose the former.

Here the main clause 'she always chose the former' may not immediately be clear, so that one has to go back to the subordinate clause to check whether 'fashionable' or 'classic' is 'the former'.

Making your sentence structure clear helps to sustain momentum. As we saw, you can sometimes do this by signalling the main points with *first, second*, etc.:

> He was promoted, first, because he showed leadership ability; second, his experience of the service was extensive; and, third, he had the 'right' family connections.

Or repeated words may be enough to signal that the items belong to the same series:

> He was promoted because of his leadership ability; because of his long experience; and because of his connections.

The more words you repeat, the heavier the emphasis. (See also under SIGNPOSTS.)

Beginning a sentence with *this*—without further specification—runs a risk of ambiguity. Similarly, an antecedent (a word referred to by a pronoun) should go before the pronoun, not after it:

> Recently, after she gave a reading in Edinburgh, I put up my friend Jean Miller from Glasgow.

Here the clause *after she gave a reading in Edinburgh* is temporarily obscure, since the reader has no idea who *she* is. Rearrangement of pronoun and antecedent makes things clearer:

> → Recently I put up my friend Jean Miller from Glasgow, after she gave a reading in Edinburgh.

Most sentences can be divided into two parts. One part, old information, reminds us of something we know already from what has gone before. The other part, the point of the sentence, conveys new information. Often the new information (the sentence's *node* or focus) is best put at the end—a word order that makes for clearer emphasis. But readers nowadays tend to have a short attention span, so don't delay unnecessarily. Delay of the node often occasions dislike of older writers:

> Like the sculptor, who never can fashion a hair or a thread in marble, the writer finds himself pulled up at many points by the nature of his material.
>
> (C. E. Montague, *A Writer's Notes on his Trade*, 1930)

Sentences can sometimes be improved by eliminating abstractions and weak, passive constructions. Older authorities such as Arthur Quiller-Couch made a strict rule of this: 'Whenever in your reading you come across one of these words, *case, instance, character, nature, condition, persuasion, degree*—whenever in writing your pen betrays you to one or another of them—pull yourself up and take thought.' He sensibly recommends, for example, replacing 'A singular degree of rarity prevails in the earlier editions of this romance' by 'The earlier editions of this romance are very rare.' On passive constructions his advice is less sound. These are often a natural choice, and they may be required for variety or because the active verb would be awkward. Passives are also preferable where the speaker is irrelevant, or matters less than the content:

It is said this poison acts very quickly.

It was decided to criminalize smoking.

Besides, a passive transformation can sometimes move an important word to the sentence end, and so give useful emphasis.

The case for simplifying structure is strong where running on of sentences has caused overloading. For example, an official announcement about refuse collection asks the public to observe that

if their refuse has not been collected on the nominated day there is no need to inform the Council as staff are aware of the areas where collections are outstanding, as these will be dealt with in due course.

This instruction could have been expressed more clearly in two simpler sentences:

→ if their refuse has not been collected on the

nominated day there is no need to inform the Council; staff are already aware which collections were postponed. These collections will be made in due course.

Even professional writers sometimes fall into something like overloading:

> These [essays] are esoteric, but charming and well written fragments on a range of topics that represent the author's personal enthusiasms—the prehistoric origins of wheat, Gregor Mendel and his peas, the discovery of DNA, the first synthesis of nitrogen fertiliser, and suchlike. (Richard H. Webb)

The reader begins to wonder how many instances are to be added. Beginning a new sentence after *enthusiasms*, and rewording, would have made for easier reading.

As we saw under PARAGRAPHS, mixing long and short sentences is often a good idea. In planning sentences, too, variety should be kept in mind. Parallel structures, such as Dr Johnson assembled in his *Rambler* essays, tend to weigh heavily on readers:

> Euphues, with great parts, and extensive knowledge, has a clouded aspect, and ungracious form . . .

If you need to use sentences with parallel elements, try to counter the effect of ponderosity with a few short, incisive sentences. But let the topic override such considerations: if you are writing about a weighty matter you can allow yourself some elaborate parallelism.

Sentences can of course take countless forms. But

probably the most important are the two large contrasting types *loose* and *periodic*. In loose sentences the main clause comes early, followed by other clauses and phrases. The loose sentence carries the day for clarity and informality, but lacks emphatic structure:

> Further on, the Rue de Turbigo crosses the Boulevard de Sébastopol, then the Rue St. Martin and the Rue Réaumur, and finally leads to the Place de la République. (Baedeker's *Paris and its Environs*)

The 'finally' tries for culminating closure; but in fact other streets could be added without greatly changing the pattern. Nothing stands out much. The loose sentence has other, very different possibilities, however:

> The 'Paul Jones's' pilot-house was a cheap, dingy, battered rattle-trap, cramped for room: but here [in the New Orleans boat] was a sumptuous glass temple; room enough to have a dance in; showy red and gold window-curtains; an imposing sofa; leather cushions and a back to the high bench where visiting pilots sit, to spin yarns and 'look at the river'; bright, fanciful 'cuspadores' instead of a broad wooden box filled with sawdust; nice new oil-cloth on the floor; a hospitable big stove for winter; a wheel as high as my head, costly with inlaid work; a wire tiller-rope; bright brass knobs for the bells; and a tidy, white-aproned, black 'texas-tender', to bring up tarts and ices and coffee during mid-watch, day and night.
>
> (Mark Twain, *Life on the Mississippi*, ch. 6)

This sentence is loose but neither careless nor shapeless.

Twain has considered the structure carefully, so that, for example, he makes the passage describing the 'Paul Jones's' cramped pilot-house short, compared with the expansive description of the New Orleans boat.

In a periodic sentence, by contrast, the main clause (and the main point) is held back until the end. There will be conditions to fulfil, qualifications to make, or causes to identify, before the consequences in the main clause follow. Periodic sentences are often ponderous, but they needn't be:

> What with lying on the rocks four days at Louisville, and some other delays, the poor old 'Paul Jones' fooled away about two weeks in making the voyage [from Cincinnati to New Orleans].

Nothing ponderous about that.

Sentences that list items present a special problem. Listing can be the most tedious procedure in the whole of writing, but it can also be an opportunity for surprise, as in the list of file card entries '*Pax Romanorum, pax vobiscum,* packs of cards, packs of hounds' (Howard Spring). Good writers have always enjoyed the challenge of making an inventory that is not dull: the most ordinary list can have pattern, surprise, and variety. In a very short list, variation is of course limited:

(1) bread, butter, jam, and cheese
(2) bread and butter and jam and cheese
(3) bread, butter, jam, cheese

These are usually taken to exhaust the possibilities. But a further, and sometimes useful, variant is

(4) bread and butter, jam and cheese

Of these, (1) is neutral, with or without the 'Oxford' comma after *jam*; (2) amplifies the number of items; (3) sets a rapid pace; and (4), like (2), conveys plenitude, and may imply categorization. If qualifiers are allowed, more can be done:

bread, unsalted butter, and excellent Mahon cheese.

And a long list can become more eventful still:

There was not at last a flower or a tree or an insect or a star in those parts, or a bird or a little beast or a fish or a toadstool or a moss or a pebble, that the little Pigtails did not know by heart.

(Walter de la Mare, *Broomsticks*)

Notice, here, how the seemingly arbitrary variations and false endings and resumptions are informed by a keen sense of rhythm. De la Mare's lists are always distinctive; you never tire of the Thief's inventory:

Not only were his plates and dishes, jugs and basins of solid gold, but so were his chair-castors, locks, keys, and bell-pulls; while his warming pans were of purest Thracian silver. (*Broomsticks*)

If any regular feature emerges, it is the interruption of listing as soon as it threatens to become routine.

Mark Twain, for all his informality, has something to teach about the forms a list can take. In his inventory of Tom Sawyer's pockets—

a lump of chalk, an indiarubber ball, three fish-hooks,

and one of that kind of marbles known as a 'sure 'nough crystal'

—each item is characterized by appropriate rhythm, phrase length, and manner of specification. (Precisely *three fish-hooks*, because if you lost count, you might be impaled.)

Even a list of names can be varied by grouping them and adding brief descriptions:

Reformers like Bentham and Godwin, apostles of reaction like Malthus, writers like Wordsworth, Coleridge, and Scott, parliamentarians like Sir James Mackintosh, the Tory cabinet members Canning and Lord Eldon, an activist like Cobbett—such figures were represented in Hazlitt's gallery.

(Laurence Stapleton, *The Elected Circle*)

The final clause after the dash gathers the whole list together and tells us what it is a list of. For some purposes, of course, this would be overelaborate. But Stapleton's interweaving of social background exemplifies a useful way of simultaneously listing items and conveying information about them.

11. Word Order

In English, much of the meaning of a sentence is conveyed through the order of its words. We expect the sequence subject–verb–object as a matter of course: 'dog bites man' means something very different from 'man bites dog'. If you are a native speaker, choosing a word order is not usually regarded as a difficult part of writing. All you need do is read a sentence over and you know at once whether the words follow a natural, idiomatic sequence. Occasionally, though, when you try to work out the best sequence for a long series of words or phrases you may find yourself at a loss. Indeed when drafting runs into difficulties the cause is surprisingly often this apparently trivial one of settling the word order. Phrases have a way of competing for the same place in the sentence. Even inside a noun phrase, placing adjectives or premodifiers is not always easy. Should it be *'black boy's shoes'* or *'boy's black shoes'*?

Sometimes ambiguity threatens, so that there is an urgent need to reorder:

Dog for sale: eats anything and is fond of children.
→ Dog for sale: fond of children. Eats anything.

For sale: antique desk suitable for lady with thick legs and large drawers.

→For sale: lady's antique desk with thick legs and large drawers.

In the simple matter of describing the place, time, manner, etc. of an event, settling the sequence of information can give disproportionate trouble. As a rule of thumb, try putting all the temporal items first, followed by the spatial. If that doesn't work, try putting the spatial items first. By such simple means, an awkward first draft—

A small crowd gathered beside the pub in Paradise Street, just after closing time, at the north end of the street

—can be much improved:

→ Just after closing time, beside the pub at the north end of Paradise Street, a small crowd gathered.

Similarly:

Imperial expansion played a central role in the foreign policies of western European nations, especially in Africa and Asia, towards the end of the Victorian period, at least in coastal regions.
→ Towards the end of the Victorian period, especially in Africa and Asia, at least in coastal regions, imperial expansion played a central role in the foreign policies of western European nations.

Often this 'temporal before spatial' plan helps to avoid the musical chairs problem—the feeling that a phrase has no place left for it.

Quite small changes in word order alter the meaning

decisively. A Victorian advertisement warns, apparently in all seriousness:

If you haven't shot yourself with Smith's ammunition you haven't lived.

The ambiguity here could have been avoided merely by transposing two words:

→ If you haven't yourself shot with Smith's ammunition you haven't lived.

In the if-clause there is now no word that could be the object of *shot*, so that the verb is taken as intransitive ('engaged in shooting'). Similar examples of misplaced words include

I need to have my hair cut badly
→ I badly need to have my hair cut.

A lecturer being prematurely made to retire
→ a lecturer being made to retire prematurely.

The extremities of a sentence particularly need thought. Next after the verb phrase, readers give most attention to a sentence's beginning and end. Locating an item at the beginning includes it in your readers' first impression; putting it at the end makes it part of the memories they take away. Ask yourself what you mean to stress, and locate it appropriately. In drafting, you can often fine-tune the word order to adjust the emphasis or clarify the meaning:

Denmark then would have the opportunity, the English feared, to once again raise the price.

→ Denmark then would have the opportunity, the English feared, to raise the price once again.

Here a minor rearrangement places the node (about repetition of the price rise 'once again') in a more emphatic position and simultaneously avoids an awkward splitting of the infinitive ('to once again raise'). By adjusting the word order quite minute effects of emphasis are possible, as in these variations:

Most of the critics of his play unfairly rubbished it.

This sequence emphasizes the severity of the critics' judgement; but, if you wish to emphasize the unfairness rather than the severity, you only have to delay 'unfairly':

Most of the critics rubbished his play, unfairly.

Again, in

His play was unfairly rubbished by most of the critics.

you are emphasizing 'most of the critics' and preparing for some such continuation as 'Only one discerned its brilliance and originality' or 'But a few of them appreciated its quality.'

Since the end of a sentence is a strategic position, reordering is sometimes needed to avoid a weak finish:

Whether a nation that now employs about one in every four workers in the public sector, and rising, can long survive an inevitable decline in its already low productivity seems unlikely.
→ It seems unlikely that a nation which now employs about one in every four workers in the public sector,

and rising, can long survive an inevitable decline in its already low productivity.

For a similar reason, putting a preposition or particle at the end of a sentence used to be considered wrong. Writers strained to construct stiffly correct sentences that avoided this terrible evil; which Winston Churchill famously ridiculed as 'a form of pedantry up with which I will no longer put'. Some computer grammar-check programs still baulk at final particles. But you should feel free to transgress this prohibition, if a final particle is the best you can come up with; 'the best you can come up with' may be a weak ending, but it is a good deal more natural than 'the best up with which you can come'. A final preposition is inevitable in

What should we talk about?

It would be impossibly stilted to put

About what should we talk?

Nowadays good writers use a word order closer to the order of spoken English than they used to. In 1967 Michael Frayn wrote

Nothing in life is as easy as it at first seems.
(*Towards the End of the Morning*)

For an intimate letter this might now be thought a shade too formal. Writing today, he might put

→ Nothing in life is as easy as it seems at first.

Within a phrase, paired items are usually arranged in ascending order of length, not importance. This principle (widespread in formal speech in Indo-European languages) was formulated in 1909 by the philologist Otto Behaghel, and so is known as 'Behagel's law of increasing members'. Hence:

> men and women
> ladies and gentlemen
> Dear Sir or Madam
> God and humankind
> man and deity

A similar principle often applies in lists; indeed, if long items are placed early in a list, the sense easily becomes fuzzy:

> When you use any of the various means of electronic communication, radio-telephone, mobile, or fax . . .
> → When you use fax, mobile, radio-telephone, or any other of the various means of electronic communication . . .

Sometimes, when there are many items of information to be conveyed together, a natural sequence can be hard to arrive at:

> . . . it was through him that was signalled the arrival in England of the Renaissance engineer.

Here the sentence ends well, but the overall sequence seems a little awkward. In such cases, reading aloud may help: how would you *say* all this in a single sentence? So perhaps one arrives at the informal, spoken language of

. . . it was through him that the arrival in England was signalled of the Renaissance engineer.

(Sir Roy Strong, The Renaissance Garden)

Here the phrases are interwoven in a way that makes for rapid, easy readability. Strictly speaking, *the arrival in England of the Renaissance engineer* is a single noun phrase. But breaking the phrase up and interweaving it with the verb *was signalled* keeps all the items in suspension until the final flourish, the important phrase *the Renaissance engineer*. Compare a similar sentence from the same author—

> That he was essentially associated with the tradition of Elizabethan and Jacobean romance can be demonstrated by the translations from the French which were dedicated to him of the *Amadis de Gaule* (1619), of *Ariana* (1636), of . . .
>
> (The Renaissance Garden)

—where the noun phrase 'translations . . . of the *Amadis*' is split to accommodate the qualifying phrase 'which were dedicated to him'.

12. Punctuation

Punctuation should not be thought of as surface decoration applied to the final draft. On the contrary it is a vital element of construction, clarifying the sense and displaying grammatical structure. It can signal parts of a sentence, announce the tone (interrogative, exclamatory), and show where the chain of discourse is leading. To omit punctuation, to insert it carelessly, to use commas monotonously: all these imply indifference to the reader.

In very early drafts, indeed, punctuation requires little attention (unless you already foresee some strategic points). Even when you are thinking about where the sentences will begin and end, you needn't put in punctuation at all: it is enough to start a new line of the draft for each provisional sentence or sentence topic. But when you sketch a continuous argument and begin to imagine someone reading the piece, it is time to put in at least the heavier stops. These help to indicate the tone and guide your reader through the paragraphs. People who don't use punctuation have to limit themselves to very short sentences, often the equivalent of a flat, expressionless voice.

The punctuation hater Rod Liddle, reviewing Lynne Truss's *Eats, Shoots and Leaves* (a manifesto for punctuation sticklers), argues that to leave out punctuation never causes any real misunderstanding. But that misses the point. Forget *real* misunderstanding: momentary misunderstanding or ambiguity is quite enough to slow readers down and spoil their pleasure. For a joke, Liddle left his review unpunctuated; the stripped-down review was supposed to show it could do without punctuation points. Instead it showed itself tedious and hard to follow, quite lacking Liddle's usual jauntiness.

Some editors try to eliminate punctuation points, especially hyphens and dashes. The colon and semicolon are under threat too; soon the comma and full stop may be left to do the work of all the other points. Then sentences will become shorter and shorter, until the comma is declared redundant. Writers who compose entirely on-screen already tend to use only the full stop, as if to say: 'I've got grammar here but I'm not going to let you know what it is.' When Picasso called punctuation the fig-leaves that hide literature's private parts he got it exactly wrong: punctuation reveals the parts of grammar and is intimately engaged with meaning.

This is not to say one should aim at an intrusive punctuation with many points. Quite the reverse: it is usually best to keep to the minimum punctuation consistent with easy reading. Written English has for a century been moving closer to spoken English, a change that has made it more readable if sometimes less exact. A milestone in this journey was the introduction of Tabloid English after about 1934: a variety with simple, often fragmentary syntax and many ellipses. Before then, as Professor Roy Harris puts it, a passer-by who saw you about to drive away might have said 'Excuse me, but do you know that the boot of your car is not properly shut?' After the 1930s, the passer-by would be more likely to say simply 'Boot's open.' Another milestone is the vogue for email, which is nearer to spoken than to written language.

Minimal punctuation goes well with the short sentences and paragraphs of popular journalism. Nevertheless a slightly fuller and heavier punctuation is best when writing for beginners, who need all the help they can get. And sometimes it is mandatory for conveying the sense accurately, as in a passage from R. F. Langley printed in *Poetry Nation Review*:

> But, as I peer at it, it opens wings and takes off, and *notiophilus* is described as 'flightless'.

The last clause is rendered meaningless by the inadequate punctuation; it should have been punctuated

> → But, as I peer at it, it opens wings and takes off. And *notiophilus* is described as 'flightless'!

All the same, light punctuation is usually preferable so long as it does not obscure the meaning.

When you are lightening punctuation, it is worth checking each item for possible ambiguity. Take out as many punctuation points as you can, then print out, and, as you read the draft through, imagine a perverse reader determined to misunderstand. Switching between delete and restore is a good way to test whether a point is needed. Many, however, find it easier to focus on punctuation in hard copy.

Punctuation points fall into three groups: stops; tone markers; and others with various special functions. The *stops* signal pauses of graduated weight or duration. They are sometimes graded in order of length, but in actuality the various stops have different functions. Their names are *comma, semicolon, colon,* and *full stop.* In the second group, *tone markers,* an interrogative tone may be marked by a *question mark* (*?*), and direct questions usually are. An excited tone used to be indicated by an *exclamation mark* (*!*). But grammarians such as H. W. Fowler, Eric Partridge, and Lynne Truss have so often warned against its overuse that it is becoming obsolete, except in graffiti and in certain mandatory special cases such as commands (*Halt!*) and exclamations otherwise ambiguous (*How useful!*). Points of the third group almost belong to spelling. Thus, an *apostrophe* marks elision, as well as indicating the possessive case, either singular (*John's* pen) or plural (*the sisters'* house). The *quotation mark* encloses direct speech (*"*). *Round brackets* or *parentheses* enclose an aside or digression, *square brackets* (US *brackets*) often enclose an authorial comment. A single *dash* indicates an interruption of sense or grammar, while two may be used to enclose a parenthesis.

Full stop. The period, full point, or full stop closes declarative sentences (those stating facts, precepts, ideas, beliefs, and feelings). The full stop can also indicate abbreviation (*A. Fowler* for *Alastair Fowler*); but this usage is obsolescent, particularly in acronyms and initialisms (UN, not U.N.), where full capitals or small capitals suffice. Three full stops (. . .) indicate *ellipsis* or omission.

Colon. The colon introduces direct speech and quotation, and also follows clauses whose sense is incomplete, to indicate that the completion follows. The words after the colon amplify, specify, or explain what the clause before it left unstated:

She disliked one thing: he would not always do what she told him.

He had a single fault, however: over-meticulousness.

The colon may be used to introduce the summing up of a list:

Ensuring that no minority group can take offence, avoiding every improper expression, checking for unobvious gender implications: all these make writing more difficult.

And some editors think the colon should wherever possible be substitued for the dash.

Semicolon. Used between the parts of a compound sentence when these are not linked by a conjunction. It makes a pause more distinct than a comma but lighter than a full stop:

The law is clear enough; the question is whether there exists the political will to apply it.

The semicolon also identifies coordinate parts of a complex sentence, and can clarify a sentence structure with many commas:

A large staff of personal secretaries, secretaries and advisors, and sub-departmental executives; and the army of public relations people, press representatives, public relations experts, and speech writers, besides those who impart spin to information; all these were not then considered necessary.

Before *which*, a semicolon indicates that the clause to follow does not qualify the immediately preceding word but rather qualifies the whole preceding clause:

> She read out the report; which was much in her favour.

This implies it was in her favour that she read out the report. Contrast:

> She read out the report, which was much in her favour

—implying that the report was favourable to her.

In complicated lists with internal punctuation the semicolon is used to indicate a new item. In British English, only a list of longish clauses is likely to need semicolons.

Comma. The comma marks a sequence of similar units (words, phrases). It is usually required between adjectives qualifying a noun:

> The brilliant, unprepared, rejected candidate gave up politics before his abilities were ever tested.

In sequences or lists the last comma (the 'Oxford comma') can sometimes be omitted:

> The screen, keyboard, and mouse
> The screen, keyboard and mouse

—but in other cases omitting it makes for ambiguity:

> the CPU, screen and keyboard and the mouse were both under guarantee.
> → the CPU, screen, and keyboard and the mouse were both under guarantee.

Occasionally a comma may be used between very closely connected main statements:

The Groke is everything that is the enemy of the sociable summer happiness of the northern valley: she is winter, she is misanthropic loneliness, she is uncontainable sadness.

(Peter Davidson, *The Idea of North*)

He knocked, he went away. That was all.

But the main clauses have to be so closely related that they would be said with the briefest of pauses between; otherwise the comma link is illegitimate, as in

He knocked, this was not the first time he had interrupted her.

Commas are often unnecessary between phrases or clauses already connected by a conjunction:

She spoke briefly, but persuasively.
→ She spoke briefly but persuasively.

Such commas shouldn't be omitted, however, without considering what shades of meaning may be altered by this. In context, the comma in the last example may imply 'you might think speaking briefly not enough; but she was so persuasive that, exceptionally, it was'. Sometimes a comma is indispensable, either for emphasis or to avoid ambiguity: *She was not failed, mercifully*. Without the comma, this would mean she was failed cruelly.

Commas are also a way of signalling a parenthesis. Parentheses, or explanatory asides, are marked by brackets, dashes, or commas. These markers are graduated in their indication: the heavier the point, the longer the explanatory sidetrip taken. The dash implies a longer parenthesis than the comma, but shorter, often, than the parenthesis that round brackets enclose. Round brackets have the convenience that the closing bracket can be followed by other punctuation. In many cases parenthetic commas are needless (as, frequently, with *of course*). In other cases they are essential:

> a literary study, embracing seventy-eight canonical and more marginal figures [implying seventy-eight canonical figures, together with a further group of marginal figures].
> → a literary study, embracing seventy-eight canonical, and more marginal, figures [implying seventy-eight figures, some of them canonical and others marginal].

You should always test the consequences of deleting parenthetic commas, since deletion may change the sense dramatically:

> The candidates who got high marks were pleased [implying that others who got low marks were not pleased].
> The candidates, who got high marks, were pleased [implying all got high marks].

Remember that parenthetic commas go in pairs: a solitary parenthetic comma can have a painfully frustrating effect:

> For all these reasons, Mycroft had concealed it—and in so doing, he had unwittingly helped his brother to discover it.　　　　(Caleb Carr, *The Italian Secretary*)

→ For all these reasons, Mycroft had concealed it—and in so doing he had unwittingly helped his brother to discover it.

Alternatively, both parenthetic commas might have been kept: 'and, in so doing, he had' etc. If you keep one comma of the pair, ambiguities are likely to creep in. Similarly with a conjunction such as *Again* (= moreover; besides), which usually requires a comma after it. But the comma may give rise to ambiguity: 'Again, the trade figures were bad.' If you mean the trade figures were repeatedly bad, put 'Again the trade figures were bad' or (sidestepping the ambiguity) 'The trade figures were again bad.'

A single *dash* can signal absence of any grammatical connection: an abrupt change of direction perhaps, or a link omitted.

> . . . when I found out, it made things harder. For me, though apparently not for Geoff, who was four years more German than me but four times more British. (Michael Frayn, *Spies*)

Here a dash before 'For me' would have helped readers; without it, they may expect a main verb, and go off on a false trail.

Hyphen. This point gives trouble disproportionate to its importance, so that Kingsley Amis advises omitting it whenever possible. Hyphens are only half as much used as they were a decade or two ago: particularly in the USA there is pressure to eliminate it altogether. Some publishers try to enforce this; but they are the publishers with no sense of incongruity, or they would surely wish to retain the hyphen at least in phrases such as

Mechanically propelled vehicle users

Man eating tiger

Problems with eating disordered patients.

Trade union reforms.

The hyphen also needs to be kept in many adjectival compounds, to avoid troubling the reader with momentary ambiguities:

Fair-haired children [as distinct from fair, bald children]
Last-ditch resistance [not the last of the ditch resistances].

Similarly with adverbs in an adjectival phrase: *well-loved author*. Hyphens are convenient for forming compound words like *radio-isotope*. When a hyphenated form becomes familiar, the hyphen is dropped and the parts fuse into one word—a process quicker in British than in American English. So, *horse-box* 1933, *horsebox* 1990 (US 1976 *horse box*); *teenager* (US 1996 *teen-ager*).

Many hyphenated words can be converted in this way to solid compounds: *to-day, today*. But take care: ambiguities can result from the consequent homophones: *re-form, reform; re-cover, recover; re-sign, resign*. Awkward cases such as 'early-sixteenth-century-warfare' are best avoided altogether (→ 'warfare of the early sixteenth century'). Interlinear hyphens can be left to the publisher—

Unfortunately so, since house rules sometimes split words ambiguously or ridiculously:

La | stresort
Not | ary public.

Famously, *notary public* was further corrupted to *not a republic*. Some stylists recommend that when you use a hyphen, you should try to use another in close proximity: somehow a solitary hyphen can seem clumsily obtrusive.

When you have finished improving the punctuation, print out and read the piece through. (And read it *aloud*; it should be a script that sounds out your meaning.) Check if the pauses are all in proportion, just as you mean them. They almost never are.

13. Quotation

Quotation has its enemies: James Boswell tells how 'Mr Wilkes censured it as pedantry. JOHNSON. "No, Sir, it is a good thing; there is a community of mind in it. Classical quotation is the *parole* [password] of literary men all over the world." ' Opposition continues: Ambrose Bierce calls quotation 'the act of repeating erroneously the words of another'; and A. S. Byatt supposes it imparts 'a kind of papery vitality and independence to, precisely, cultural clichés cut free from the web of language that gives them precise meaning'. All the same, quotation is a chief resource for a writer; it just needs to be used judiciously, taking into account context, readership, and immediate purpose.

The commonest purpose is to illustrate or exemplify. To illustrate Kingsley Amis's acquaintance with Robert Graves, one might quote a letter of Amis's:

> In 1963 Kingsley Amis leased a house on Mallorca, and got to know Robert Graves: 'Graves . . . has been in most amiable form. His best stroke to date has been to tell us, on the morning of the house-signing-up, that the place had burned down in the night, revealing after a minute or two that it was April Fools' Day'.
>
> (To William Rukeyser, 2 April 1963)

Demonstration—a modern equivalent of medieval proof by authority—is another common aim of quotation, but one to pursue with care, as we shall see. Quotation can also make for interest, by adding pungency of language, perhaps, or at least a different voice.

Without doubt, quotation can raise the calibre of writing by a quantum leap. In Thomas Peacock's *Crochet Castle*, Dr Folliott goes so far as to say that 'a book that furnishes no quotations is, *me iudice* [in my judgement], no book— it is a plaything'. And Dr Johnson goes almost as far: 'if the authors cited be good, there is at least so much worth reading in the book of him who quotes them'. Here Johnson comes close to acknowledging the danger that quotation may show up your own writing as inferior. Montaigne tells how in his reading he came upon a passage from a clas- sical author: 'I had dragged along languidly after French words so bloodless, fleshless, and empty of matter and sense that they really were nothing but French words. At the end of a long and tedious road, I came upon a passage that was sublime, rich, and lofty as the clouds.' This clas- sical quotation 'was a precipice so straight and steep that after the first six words I realized that I was flying off into another world'. He sees the risk, for he adds, 'If I stuffed one of my chapters with these rich spoils, it would show up too clearly the stupidity of the others.' Paraphrase of the ancients, as distinct from quotation, would never have challenged Montaigne to raise his sights like this.

Quoting to prove things, however, conceals a far greater danger. Especially in literary criticism, quotation is often used to demonstrate a point, as if the point could be made automatically just by the presence of the quotation—as if the quotation was self-evidently on the writer's side. Well, quoting may indeed help to support your argument. But that will not happen automatically; you will have to show exactly how the quotation helps your case. So it is best to introduce a quotation, especially a long quotation, by saying what you hope it will show, spelling out exactly how it is relevant:

Smith clearly implies as much, when she writes . . .

Such a preliminary can serve as a topic sentence, relating a quoted paragraph to the one before, or to the argument of the whole piece. It prepares readers in a general way to expect in the quotation what you hope they will find there. Better still is the introduction that summarizes the content of the quotation:

The boy's father, Mr Pendyce, is a collector: 'His collection of rare, almost extinct birds' eggs was one of the finest in the "three kingdoms" '.

(Kermode, *Pieces of My Mind*)

After the introduction comes a transition to the quotation itself: here the transition is simply the colon after *collector*. And, when the quotation has been made, even then, in argumentative writing, demonstration is not finished. (F. R. Leavis, notoriously, tended to assume it was: that quotation would do all the work of persuasion—'There is no need to explain at length'; 'I leave the reader to look up, if he likes, the two speeches.') No, you have still to draw out from the quotation the specific points you mean it to illustrate, analysing or at least discussing them. Then, at last, you are entitled to come to reasoned conclusions. As a rule of thumb, your own words about a quotation are likely to be as many as those of the quotation itself.

If an indented quotation seems too long, you can usually break it up by putting a phrase or two into your own words. (Interrupt as early in the quotation as you can.) These paraphrased parts, which are not indented, change the whole appearance of the page. And your paraphrase can guide readers to take up from the parts directly quoted just what you mean them to take:

> Chesterton gets some strikingly stagy effects:
> the seven top anarchists meet on the glassed-in
> balcony of a Leicester Square restaurant and
> observe on the street below them not only a
> policeman, 'pillar of common sense and order',
> but also the poor, entertained by a barrel organ
> and full of the vivacity, vulgarity, and irrational
> valour of those 'who in all those unclean streets
> were . . . clinging to the decencies and charities of
> Christendom'.
>
> (Kermode, *Pieces of My Mind*)

Here the paraphrase in simpler language prepares readers for the more abstract phrase 'decencies and charities'.

When should you quote? Not, usually, in the very first sentence of a paragraph. But quotation can often be used as a disguised restatement or development of the topic sentence. No point is fully made until illustrated or exemplified, and, for this, quotation is well adapted. It can for example introduce a famous instance, and in doing so implicitly suggest the original author is on your side of the argument.

Again, you can pit quotations against one another like proverbs:

The Duke of Wellington is said to have advised a new MP, 'Don't quote Latin; say what you have to say, and then sit down'. But Charles James Fox gave opposite advice: 'No Greek; as much Latin as you like; and never French under any circumstances. No English poet unless he has completed his century'.

(Attributed to Fox in Benjamin Disraeli, *Endymion* (1880), ch. 76)

Too much of this ventroloquism, however, can seem evasive, as if you are avoiding commitment in your own person.

To splice a quotation into your piece, no more than a comma or colon is absolutely necessary—if that. Just as often, though, you may make things clearer if you use some such introduction as: 'X writes'; 'according to X'; 'as X has it'; 'X puts it well when she says'; 'X argues that, in her words . . .'; 'but X disagrees, implausibly arguing that . . .' If the quotation is very short it can be put as a parenthesis. Or you can give its source as a parenthesis:

'Come let me write', the lover says in 34, 'And to what end?'

'Come let me write' (the lover says in 34) 'And to what end?'

To give maximum salience to a strong quotation, you can withhold its source, then give it afterwards casually, for the surprise:

it is interesting to recall the remarks of an American who saw the place [Coventry] in 1855: '. . . this antiquity is so massive that there seems to be no means of getting rid of it without tearing society to pieces'. A process which Mr Nathaniel Hawthorne did not live to see. (Sir John Summerson, *Heavenly Mansions*)

Some write as if quotation were elitist in itself—and elitist in a bad sense. This is not a new idea, as the passage from Boswell that I began with shows. But the politics of quotation are far from simple. Radicals, progressives, populists, writers of the left: all like to quote those who support their view. True, Fox advised against quotation from the Greek; but that was in a period of educational decline. The question of propriety largely resolves itself into one of readership: will your readers recognize the quotation and appreciate it? The answer doesn't turn simply on social class: it depends more on education. Quoting Greek or Latin may be *intellectually* elitist; in *How to Be an Alien* George Mikes says, 'In England only uneducated people show off their knowledge; nobody quotes Latin or Greek authors in the course of conversation, unless he has never read them.' The current antipathy to quotation may be a failure of nerve, consequent on dumbing-down. John Selden the seventeenth-century Parliamentarian seems to give good advice: 'In quoting of books, quote such authors as are usually read; others you may read for your own satisfaction, but not name them.' But turning away from quotation may be tantamount to flinching from the entire challenge of tradition. And things change: I know some young people who show signs of being better read than their teachers.

Besides, it isn't always obvious when a writer is quoting. Many apparent quotations are nothing of the sort, but phrases or lines that have been assimilated into the language, as often as not from Pope or Shakespeare (both notoriously 'full of quotations'). How many of those you hear saying 'more will mean less' consciously quote Kingsley Amis? 'Life is theatrical', said Emerson, 'and literature a quotation.' Samuel Beckett's later work amply confirms that. Quotation blurs into echo whenever widely read people write; for they seldom quote accurately— 'Misquotation is the pride and privilege of the learned.' When he wrote this, Hesketh Pearson the biographer probably meant that the words well-read people quote are so familiar to them that they use them as their own. So quotation shades off into cliché, formula, or proverb the quotation of the people. To be happy about cliché but censorious about quotation might be thought arbitrary.

Suppose you decide, All right, I will quote, how then are you to find a quotation that fits? Some advise that if you need to look for a quotation, you shouldn't: quotations should come spontaneously to mind from memory. Others see quotation as a natural advantage of note-taking or commonplace-book compiling. But, if you haven't formed the habit of taking notes or practising memory art, you may find apt quotations elusive. You may have no more than a vague inkling of a quotation that might be apt if you could only remember it. That's when reference books and databases come into their own. Sir Winston Churchill writes 'It is a good thing for an uneducated man to read books of quotations.' That may sound patronizing—until you discover he is referring to himself. See further under REFERENCE BOOKS.

When you find a suitable quotation, you haven't finished until you look it up and make sure of its exact meaning in context. (Quotation has a way of showing up the quoter's ignorance.) Besides, some databases have a low standard of accuracy; scanning from a good original text is better than downloading from a bad one.

Whatever you do, quote sparingly. You don't want the piece to come over as a bunch of quotations to which you have only added the elastic. The quotations should never seem the real meat, with your contribution merely the connective tissue.

Long quotations—more than four lines or about thirty-five words—are indented, without quotation marks. Short quotations—words or phrases—can be enclosed within quotation marks and subordinated to the sentence.

> The publishers describe this book as 'lean', which may be taken to refer to its style, though it also serves as a euphemism for 'very short, especially considering the price'. (Kermode, *Pieces of My Mind*)

If you quote a complete sentence, introduce it with a colon but begin it with a capital.

14. Originality

How do you find what to say? Obviously by reading and thinking and note-taking. But the doubt may arise whether ideas from books are truly your own ideas. Someone is sure to ask nervously 'Shouldn't I be writing original ideas?' Well, very few if any of our ideas and words can be called our own. We came into the world without them, and have unconsciously taken them over from forgotten sources: parents, teachers, role models, books, and the Internet. Dante was partly aware of this: 'Speech is what we acquire without any rule, by imitating our nurses' (*De Vulgari Eloquentia*). Once we assimilate ideas we normally forget where they came from; they are ours now, even if not uniquely so.

'Surely' (you rightly worry) 'that opens the door to plagiarism? I know when I have ideas, or don't; and I want to express them in my own words, not someone else's.' Think what you've just said: is the phrase *my own* specially yours? Of course not; each word 'in common use' is common property. So, too, with idioms and clichés and verbal formulas and commonplace metaphors and ordinary ways of putting things. If you write in a tradition—and you'd better, if you want anyone to understand you—you can't help borrowing ideas and words. Even the most original writers use conventions of description, narrative, listing, argument, etc. You only plagiarize if you steal a complex of ideas together with their verbal expression and pass them off as your own. Specifically, you are guilty of plagiarism only if you leave your loot unchanged, if it is recognizable enough to provide evidence for a lawsuit (see Halsbury's *Laws of England*, 'Copyright, design right and related rights', 2 (1) iii. 64). To keep on the right side of the law (and the examiners), you must thoroughly appropriate what you borrow. Lorenzo Valla, a Renaissance humanist, half-seriously advised writers to steal; he meant to recommend imitation of the great writers of the past. That was good but dangerous advice: downloading chunks from the Internet is not what Valla had in mind. If you steal brick and reset it as marble, well and good—but only if you have worked hard to make the 'borrowed' ideas your own.

How is that to be done? In brief, you have to assimilate the borrowings by incorporating them into your own thinking. You must fit them into your personal schemes of thought and completely reformulate them using your own words. Then, perhaps, you select the best passages and make them even better. Next you apply them, so that they are fully relevant to your piece, rephrasing them in words appropriate to your especial purpose. But always remember: changing the words alone isn't enough; you have to make the content your own as well. As you refine the passages, reshaping and adapting them, you will find yourself disagreeing and modifying and perhaps modernizing them. This coming to grips with other texts is what to focus on. When you are required to credit your sources for an academic paper, this isn't just to catch you out, but to let you show how much work you've done. Tom

Sawyer's aunt began family worship 'with a prayer built from the ground up of solid courses of scriptural quotations, welded together with a thin mortar of originality'. Your mortar has to be a good deal thicker than that.

Ask yourself if you fully understand the point you're taking over, and, if not, work on it some more. Have you made the imitated passage fully consistent with the new context? (Transferring an idea from one field to another is not easy, and may be a very original thing to do.) Have you subordinated the borrowing to your own argument? Have all your changes been improvements? The changes should go far beyond individual words. You can change the scale (going into more detail usually entails fresh thought); the point of view (descriptive to critical, etc.); and many other features. Compression might make the original more concise; enlargement might allow you to introduce new details, and so invent fresh contents. Translating *Gargantua and Pantagruel*, Sir Thomas Urquhart consistently expands Rabelais's lists to include extra items—and is praised for his originality. When you follow another passage, think of what you are writing as an undisguised, legitimate imitation, a perfectly respectable activity. Montaigne, most original of sixteenth-century Frenchmen, largely constructed his essays out of quotations of the ancients—nearly 1,300 of them. Much Renaissance literature, including Shakespeare's plays, was produced in just this way; and much recent literature too.

Among many ways of imitation, you can use the *exploratory* strategy of discovering your own view by avoiding everything in the original. You treat it merely as a point of departure, distancing yourself from it wherever possible. Without denying its use as a source of ideas or words, you ignore the sense of the original and boldly take up a different stance altogether. Another way is the *dialectical* strategy of contending with your model by emulating it, or rejecting it through parody or travesty. And in *exploitative* imitation you treat the model as no more than a convenient quarry for materials—an allusion here, a quotation there.

Learn to imitate authors consciously, so as to know when you're not copying them unconsciously. If you know how you're changing a model—exactly what you're doing with its ideas—then it may become a resource of your own.

Suppose you want to use a Coleridgean passage on 'the hooks and eyes of intellectual memory', but already have too many direct quotations, and anyway the phrase seems a bit trivial (as it did to Coleridge himself). So you want to aim at a paraphrase that keeps the flavour of the original. You could try focusing on his choice of words, which through dictionaries and footnotes would lead you to Quintilian's comparison of memory with fishing, to the medieval trope of the fishhook as a symbol of memory art, and to Petrarch's advice that 'when you come to any passages that seem to you useful, impress secure marks against them, which may serve as hooks in your memory'. A book on the art of memory explains that 'in a properly designed memory ... the source will be like a line with many hooks on it, and as one pulls in one part of it, all the fish will come along' (Mary Carruthers). From this a footnote takes you to Joseph Glanvill, a source of Arnold's Scholar-Gipsy, who imagined the material particles of memory as grappling one other in an intricate tangle by 'hooks' and 'hooklets'. Then you recall that Locke's theory of 'association' famously developed similar ideas, and you track down a typical instance in a book of seventeenth-century thought. So you finally arrive at a phrase of your own, *fish-hooks of memory's association*. Notice what has been going on here: by focusing on Coleridge's words you have traced his ideas back to a tradition, if not his actual source. And you have also ended up with not a bad phrase for your piece. Of course your own route might be quite different; but the principle remains the same. Research, hard detective work, and purposeful drafting almost inevitably lead to original serendipities.

To assimilate someone else's view, start by comparing it with other writers' views, to get it into perspective (a perspective the original author may not have had). Next, evaluate the view, and decide whether you share it and find it authoritative; if you see flaws, remove them. Then replace every feature of the original passage—the examples, references, evidence, quotations, arguments— with features of your own. Next, eliminate all the words of the model. The way to be original is not to express an idea no one else has ever had (unlikely, perhaps impossible). Rather is it to follow up old ideas that are still true in your own situation, and to work on assimilating and expressing them as thoroughly as you can. Honest writing always involves hard thinking: there are no shortcuts to originality. Certainly waiting for inspiration won't get you there.

In student writing, the question of originality has a special complexion. Here attribution is everything: imitation has to be kept transparent at all times. To cheat by concealing the sources constitutes a grave offence, and warrants automatic failure if not expulsion. Such plagiarism is also self-defeating, since it deprives the offender of the chance to learn from the exercise by completing it honestly.

15. Readers

Writing comes more easily if the piece is for a group you know, perhaps even belong to; who will be receptive, you hope—or, at worst, who are likely to object in ways you can anticipate and prepare for. When you don't know your audience it is harder to imagine them. This difficult stretch of the imagination is best left until you have finished a few drafts. Until then, forget about readers: the attempt to realize them can be daunting, if not inhibiting. In any event, the earliest drafts need to be author-centred, since you are trying to discover in them what you yourself have to say. Concentrate at first on getting your own views into focus and defending them.

Later, when your piece is a little further advanced, when you are drafting paragraphs in detail and choosing words, the focus changes. It is time to turn towards your readers, whose needs must dominate the writing of all later drafts. After every paragraph, now, you should ask yourself how relevant it is to the interests of readers, and how it will be received.

The present chapter may be the most necessary of all, especially for a beginner. Good writers may simply be those who imagine their readers best and keep their readers' needs in mind most continuously. If you have potential readers in focus, accessibility can't be in doubt, nor your tone and clarity. Start asking yourself, Will readers understand this? Will they take that the right way? Will this be ambiguous to them? Are they challenged enough here, or too much? Always gauge the reader's probable level of knowledge and intelligence: don't say anything obscure without adding an early explanation. Do it tactfully, though, perhaps disguising the explanation as an alternative word. *Hypostatize, or reify* might be acceptable for one (very specialist) audience; for another audience, it might work better to abandon the technical term and cut straight to the explanation: *treat as a concrete thing*. But then you also have to consider if too much has been explained: is the sentence patronizing? Insultingly obvious?

Imagine readers to be more moral and intelligent than yourself, yet hard to convince, sceptical, and inclined to misread everything you write. In argumentative writing, have in mind ideological opponents, or else literalists deaf to all suggestion except the most carefully phrased. If these perpetual imaginings seem too elusive, you could try writing for a real person you know: imagine reading your draft to this person, and you may hit the right tone quite readily. Don't choose a like-minded friend, however; it's all too easy to convince oneself and build castles in the air that crumble at the first breath of independent criticism. Better assume the worst, and write with ideological opponents in mind.

Writing for yourself has hopefully led to precise expression. But that's not enough; you have also to be clear to others. And not just clear: the piece has to be easy and enjoyable to read. If possible, get feedback from friends. Their comments may well shock you; but swallow your pride and avoid any hint of defensiveness. The more negative their criticisms, the greater their potential contribution—if you take the criticisms on board and make appropriate adjustments.

If the piece is a review, added complications enter in, since there are in effect two distinct readerships: the readers of the journal you are writing for constitute one readership, the author under review another. The thought of the author reading your criticisms can be alarming, especially if the review is very adverse. You may be tempted to dispel this feeling by ignoring its cause: by, as it were, denying the author's existence. That is not advisable; it tends to produce an excessively hostile, aggressive review. Such reviews are only justifiable if the work reviewed is fraudulent or culpably inaccurate. Then it is time to have fun; as Auden says, 'one cannot review a bad book without showing off'. Usually the best plan is to keep the author in mind and temper your criticisms, avoiding unnecessary offence and preserving a courteous tone. That may help you to think of magnanimous qualifications, and so to arrive at balanced judgements. If you aren't up to this, you may have to fall back on E. M. Forster's defence: 'no author has any right to whine. He was not obliged to be an author. He invited publicity, and he must take the publicity that comes along'.

In expository prose—explaining or describing—readers need to be given information in a helpful sequence. Never depend on their knowing anything you have not yet explained. To arrange this you have to keep readers in mind at each stage. Look how Sir Winston Churchill does it in *A History of the English Speaking Peoples* (a book meant for the general reader, intelligent but not academic in a specialized sense):

> In the summer of the Roman year 699, now described as the year 55 before the birth of Christ, the Proconsul of Gaul, Gaius Julius Caesar, turned his gaze upon Britain. (Churchill, *The Birth of Britain*)

When he wrote this, in 1956, Churchill could assume knowledge of the date 55 BC: every schoolboy knew that then. But to start in the obvious way with the known, familiar date would not have best served Churchill's purpose. He wanted to suggest a Roman perspective, in which of course the Christian calendar would be out of place; so he begins instead with the ancient notation. But the Roman date might be misunderstood as 699 BC or AD, so he adds a specification: *now described as the year 55 before the birth of Christ*. This entails a longish rigmarole, but it unobtrusively accomplishes a good deal. The next phrase, *the Proconsul of Gaul* (rather than 'Julius Caesar'), again takes up a Roman viewpoint: to them, Gaius Julius Caesar was only one of a long series of proconsuls. In this opening sentence, then, readers learn (or are reminded of) the Roman reckoning of the date; Julius Caesar's Proconsulship; and his full Latin name. Such rapid intake of old and new information, integrated into a perspective view, can give readers a keen pleasure.

Elaborating the Roman viewpoint further, Churchill explains how Julius Caesar thought of Britain:

> To Caesar, the Island now presented itself as an integral

part of his task of subjugating the Northern barbarians to the rule and system of Rome. The land not covered by forest or marsh was verdant and fertile. The climate, though far from genial, was equable and healthy. The natives, though uncouth, had a certain value as slaves for rougher work on the land, in mines, and even about the house. There was talk of a pearl fishery, and also of gold.

Here a host of particulars—land forested, marshy, or 'verdant and fertile'; climate uncongenial to a southerner but temperate and healthy; natives uncouth but valuably performing various graded labours—are made intelligible and memorable by arranging them in structured patterns. And a slave hierarchy is indirectly evoked by the phrase *even about the house*. All this is imagined from Caesar's viewpoint, which readers are invited temporarily to share.

A similar structural patterning organizes Churchill's account of the Viking longship and its use:

Such was the vessel which, in many different sizes, bore the Vikings to the plunder of the civilised world—to the assault of Constantinople, to the siege of Paris, to the foundation of Dublin, and the discovery of America. Its picture rises before us vivid and bright: the finely carved, dragon-shaped prow; the high, curving stern; the long row of shields, black and yellow alternately, ranged along the sides; the gleam of steel; the scent of murder.   (Churchill, *The Birth of Britain*)

The repeated schemes on the plan *the X of Y* (as in 'the

assault of Constantinople' and 'the siege of Paris') are simple enough to be taken up rapidly, even if some readers didn't previously know, for example, that the Vikings besieged Paris. The familiar appearance of the longship is sharpened by sensory details ('shields, black and yellow alternately'), and the sequence 'assault . . . siege . . . foundation . . . discovery' prepares readers for the expansive 'great ocean voyages' in the next sentence. The vivid particulars are not without variety and surprise, as in the unexpected 'scent of murder'. All rhetoric? Doubtless; but we are bound to speak and write rhetoric all the time; the choice is between good rhetoric and bad.

Suppose you are reporting a football match. In this kind of writing you can take much for granted about your readers. They won't need you to tell them there were eleven players on each side (unless one was sent or carried off). And you can assume they know the main rules; although you may have to touch on intricacies of the offside rule if there was a disputed ruling. If the match was an important one, readers will probably know the score but expect you to detail the scorers and timing of goals. You can also assume knowledge of a club's past form. What topics are left? Readers will want to hear of disputed fouls, deflected shots, injuries actual or acted, cards red or yellow. Changes to the line-up may call for comment, team performances, levels of fitness, the success of individual players, or substitutions during the game. Your general impressions of the game will be expected. If (as often) a good result has generated excessive euphoria, you may wish to distinguish between result and performance, and try to restore a sense of proportion. Or there may be gossip about prospective transfers to discuss (your readers require you to be something of a soothsayer). Finally you must give an insider's report of the team managers' reactions.

Thinking of your readers is not just a matter of answering expectations or selecting an appropriate level of discourse. Different kinds of writing affect readers differently, and this needs to be planned. Most non-fiction obviously consists of explanation (exposition), argument, and description; but another ingredient, narrative, should not be forgotten. Storytelling may seem to belong rather with fiction. But any report is liable to call for an account of a situation, and the account is often best given in the form of a narrative. Narrative can be more informative than discursive generalities—and less soporific.

So far, readers have been imagined as in need of instruction or else as superior, critical, captious. But you also have it in your power to imagine them in another, equally valuable way. You can imagine your readers as enjoying what you write. But you can only make it pleasurable to them in actuality if you enter into their preferences. What are readers likely to enjoy?

One thing they will surely take pleasure in is clarity: people like to understand what they read, and understand it easily, understand without making efforts to construe difficult syntax. They don't want to be puzzled unnecessarily or have to fight their way through hordes of unfamiliar names and words. This needn't mean dumbing down, for example by omitting all unfamiliar names: most people like to be informed of writers they should know about. And unusual words needn't be avoided: they can be unobtrusively accompanied with explanations. Most readers positively enjoy the feeling of lively enlightenment, of taking in new information rapidly (see PERFORMANCE AND CONCURRENCE). They also enjoy the small thrill of surprise, as when a sentence ends on an unexpected note. At the same time, they like familiar, expected things; so it is best of all to mix the strange with the ordinary. Patterned sentences give the satisfaction of expectations fulfilled: the sequence

> missing links, the disappeared, soldiers missing in action

reads less well than

> → missing links, missing persons, soldiers missing in action.

Descriptive reports may seem relatively independent of considerations of reader response. But description can vary from boring to exciting, according to how well its readers have been imagined. An exclusively author-centred approach will seldom succeed in giving a lifelike account of people, places, or events. At the very least you need to take different interests into account: describe a social event exclusively in terms of the celebrities encountered, and you will leave some readers cold. It may help to aim at a mix of impessions relating to different faculties or senses, in the hope of accommodating readers of various temperaments. Try combining auditory with visual images, or evocation of scents and textures. Indirect description can work best of all, using literary allusion, perhaps, or fashion terms. Was the party noisy? Crowded? Was it a Prada sort of occasion, or more Top Shop? Exaggerated tropes are a useful resource: 'the noise was coming up our legs and playing us like bass fiddles'. Even grammar can supply a figure:

> I was only 17, had hardly one adverbial clause to my
> name . . .   (Albert Morris)

And don't forget to throw in an occasional arbitrary detail, just for its pungent flavour.

If you are writing a familiar letter, imagine the topics likely to give your correspondent pleasure. Among the 'paramount topics' for a letter, according to Michael Collier in the *Georgia Review*, are 'books, writing, reading, and childhood . . . followed by wives, children and friends, and then in no particular order cats, dogs, birds, gardens, domestic arrangements, music, museums and their current exhibitions'. To this list you might add gossip, comments on your friend's previous letter, and reminders of shared experience. Political news, on the other hand, merits little space (unless in correspondence between politicians); it will be stale by the time it is read. Try to bring your correspondent nearer by giving close-up details of an immediate scene; the best letter I ever had from a writer (now dead) simply recounted particulars of how, in age, he spent his time throughout the day.

16. Words

In your earliest drafts you may not have thought much about words—using shorthand instead, abbreviations, symbols, and other temporary stand-ins. Those drafts were private, unintelligible to anyone but yourself. Now you can write a draft using actual words, to work out your thinking in detail and body it into language. This draft is still private, so you are free to use any words you like.

For this first fully verbalized draft you will need all the variety of language at your disposal: an abundance of phrases, idioms, clichés, quotations, associations, and familiar expressions. Return yet again to your notes and previous drafts, but this time begin to attend to the language as well as the ideas. Call up words from your reading for the piece, until you get a sense of lexical profusion. Enjoy the wealth of words related to the topic—all of it available for the piece. If you need more, you might look up a few of the keywords in a large dictionary or encyclopedia or dictionary of quotations (see under REFERENCE BOOKS). Or open a *thesaurus* ('treasure chest') and weigh the lexical coins it contains. Suppose your subject is promotion. Collins's *Roget's International Thesaurus* has this entry on 'Promotion, demotion':

NOUNS 1. Promotion, preferment, advancement, advance,

boost [colloquial], raise, elevation, upgrading; exaltation, aggrandizement; ennoblement; graduation, passing.

2. demotion, degrading, downgrading, debasement, abasement, reduction, Irish promotion [jocular]; bump, bust [both slang].

VERBS 3. Promote, prefer, advance, boost [colloquial], raise, elevate, upgrade; kick upstairs [jocular]; exalt, aggrandize; ennoble, knight, esquire; pass, graduate.

4. demote, degrade, downgrade, debase, abase, reduce, lower, give an Irish promotion [jocular]; bump, bust [both slang].

Here you have a whole range of alternative words, and can glimpse ways to shift from nominal to verbal expression (*preferment, prefer*). Several words are listed as *colloquial* or *jocular*; suggesting the different levels of formality accessible. Other words may be listed as *obsolete*; prompting you to add your own updated alternatives. In short, this is a semantic domain where you are likely to find the exact words you need.

Moreover the alternatives in a thesaurus may suggest relevant metaphors, distinctions, or even new approaches. In *Stevenson's Book of Quotations*, under the heading 'Success', appears the biblical text 'Promotion cometh neither from the east, nor from the west, nor from the south', which might open up a further route into your topic. So might this subversive entry in Ambrose Bierce's *The Devil's Dictionary*: 'Promote, verb. In financial affairs, to contribute to the development of a transfer company—one that transfers money from the pocket of the investor to that of the promoter.'

Before choosing words (or phrases, which are commoner than solitary words), you should mull over the options. Distinguish big words from little, large from small, long from short, rare from ordinary. Is this word suave enough for the purpose? Is that one too rough? And is that other word altogether fluent? Does it suggest dense complication? Or does it feel sensuous? Cool? Precise? Say the word and distinguish its sound: is it resonant, or soft, or attenuated? Many writers gather useful words and phrases into a commonplace-book of their own. Edmund Wilson, the anglophobe critic and novelist, collected serviceable descriptive colour words. But if you invest in that plan you will need to draw on your lexical reserves with care. Wilson's mistress would not have liked him to call her eyes *benzoazurine* (if she wasn't a chemist) or *bleu Louise* (if her name was Loreen) or *old blue* (if she was of a certain age).

When you choose a word, have in mind both general and particular considerations. In general, prefer small, ordinary words to unusual, portentous ones. Big words run the risk of pomposity:

> If you wish to switch the functionality off altogether
> → If you wish to switch the function off altogether
>
> Readers will have seen the signage and roadworks.
> → Readers will have seen the signs and roadworks.

The Midas touch of officialdom turns every word to wood:

> Investing resources into a newly formed Capacity, Building, and Research team to directly inform and develop its Commissioning Strategy and Service Development

→ Investing in a new planning committee.

Even when spoken diction is used, pretentiousness easily falls into incoherence:

> I would say that looking to the objective end, I think there would be a fruitful discussion and in that the man has written three books and I guess in that respect having a body of information out there.

In choosing words, the criteria depend on the sort of piece you plan. Is it to be easy, readable, transparent? Or, do you want to draw your readers into the difficulties of the subject and force them to come to grips with your specialism? The former plan is usually preferable.

Next you may consider if a word is in context natural, idiomatic, and obvious, or draws attention to itself undesirably. Clichés (*the bottom line*) and formulas (*of course*) are the most obvious materials for constructing sentences; by all means use them until you find something better. The trouble with clichés is that being overused they soon become disgusting. When you gain experience as a writer, however, you may occasionally be able to finesse the standard cliché: instead of accepting it just as it comes to mind (or appears in the thesaurus), you can once in a while turn a phrase by departing slightly from the standard form. If 'he had a voice like a foghorn' seems played out, you can try 'his voice sounded like a horn in the fog'.

Although you should most often choose common, unremarkable language, from time to time you may want to foreground a phrase, perhaps to point up the mood, perhaps just to avoid featurelessness. If a Scot were composing a letter to an English friend about how, just as he was sitting down to an al fresco meal, over the Salisbury Crags poured a sea mist, he would not call it a *haar* (the proper word), in case that might be obscure. (Unless he meant to instruct, or convey the mist's alien intrusiveness.) But later on in the same letter from Edinburgh, he might well mention a sudden *avatar* of hot-air balloons above his garden wall. The foregrounded word (more usual in theological discourse) would suit the balloons' marvellous appearance.

If your topic has its own technical vocabulary, you may wish to use precise wording. You can easily find the correct terms in specialized dictionaries (for nautical terms there is *The Oxford Companion to the Sea*, or H. Paasch's multilingual dictionary *From Keel to Truck*). But watch out! Precision runs the risk of pedantry, and the more specialized your diction the further you remove yourself from ordinary readers. Keep your purpose in mind: is it to help readers to a clear understanding, or to show off how much you know about martingales? Even T. S. Eliot tried for 'the formal word precise but not pedantic'. Don't be like Eliot's Sweeney and take the line

> I gotta use words when I talk to you
> But if you understand or if you don't
> That's nothing to me and nothing to you . . .
> (Eliot, 'Fragment of an Agon')

Still, it won't do to be sloppy. Always prefer the right to the wrong word. Between pairs of similar words, for example, you really must choose the one you mean. *Continuous* and *continual; continual* and *perpetual; per-*

petual and *persistent; persist* and *survive; opposite* and *obverse; immigrant* and *emigrant; intuition* and *instinct; embed* and *enfold; engraft* and *entwine*: these do not mean the same. (Other pairs of words that can give difficulty are listed in the chapter on CORRECTNESS.) Such pairs need to be looked up in a dictionary and carefully distinguished before you make your choice. Dictionaries of usage are specially helpful for this (see REFERENCE BOOKS).

Some individual words are a little tricky to use; they conceal traps, easily enough avoided but requiring care. *Unique*, for example, is an all-or-nothing qualifier: a thing can't be 'very unique' or 'somewhat unique'; it simply is, or is not, unique. Similarly with *protagonist* (derived from Greek words meaning 'first actor'): strictly speaking a play or novel can only have one protagonist, or chief character. *Chief protagonist* and *all the protagonists* are solecisms. *Criterion* is another tricky word: its plural *criteria* is often used, wrongly, as a singular. Again, sticklers used to insist there could only be *two alternatives*; but for more than a century it has been considered correct to speak of multiple alternatives. Nevertheless the narrower meaning of *alternative* persists, so that a doubt hangs over the cosmologist Stephen Hawking's question 'Why ... should a man be sent to jail for robbing a bank when he had no other alternative?' Is 'other' superfluous? Did the man have no choice at all? Or does 'no other alternative' imply that the man had two choices, of which robbing the bank was one?— that he had 'no other alternative' than the alternative of not robbing it?

In choosing words many criteria, many norms, should be kept in mind. Is this word too informal? Is that word easy enough to be quite clear? Is that other too noticeable? Slang is sometimes quite acceptable, but its merits need to be considered in individual instances; its use calls for a definite choice. Wherever possible, avoid evanescent jargon and fashionable buzzwords, such as *to impact*. Similarly we can do without ugly verbs mass-produced from nouns: *to dialogue; to version; to resource; to reference*; and *to legend*. They are ugly, and become uglier still: *to interface; to incentivize; to bottom-line*. Coinages take their chances; some live and others die. For sometimes they show creativity in face of rapid change: *ideopolis*, for example. But usually their reckless frequency and awkwardness suggests that the perpetrator finds it less trouble to invent a word than find one. Surely we have no need of *standees, crapness, pre-disastered,* or *non-doorsteppable*? Faced with convenient new words you shouldn't be too disgusted-of-Tunbridge-Wells to use them; but you needn't be allured by them either.

You may have favourite words, words you like so much you want to get them in at all costs. If so, it's a good idea consciously to avoid them. (They'll creep in often enough, without your noticing.) It's what you mean that must determine which words you use. For example does anyone ever truly mean *opined*? This word has long been regarded as ludicrously stilted (except when used to signal contempt for another's view); the current move to reinstate it is surely doomed.

17. Metaphors

Metaphors describe one thing in terms of another. To write a sentence free from metaphor of any kind would be almost impossible: it underlies every idiom. *These answers fall into two groups* does not mean the answers literally take a tumble. The most prosaic utterances are likely to abound in figures of this vestigial sort:

> She soon changed her tune when I won the lottery.
>
> His manager warned him not to rock the boat.
>
> In the long run it's better to buy than rent.
>
> The potential downside of tax reduction.

Such transparent, faded, or *dead metaphors* (metaphors so familiar as to be no longer felt as figurative) are paradoxically the living stuff of language. They offer a resource you need do nothing special to activate. Occasionally you can contribute by introducing a new metaphor of your own, or bringing a dead one to life. That is worth doing, for, as Addison of *The Spectator* says, 'A noble Metaphor, when it is placed to an Advantage, casts a kind of Glory round it, and darts a Lustre through a whole sentence.' Metaphors clarify ideas, make them memorable, and give the reader a pleasurable sense of discovery.

If you wrote that 'Yeats and Pound were two sides of the same coin', the metaphor of a coin would be a wornout cliché, stone dead. As dead as a doornail. But if you were to dwell a little on the coin image, the metaphor might still be galvanized:

Yeats and Pound were two sides of the same rare coin.

Working out this figure, the reader participates in finding its sense by tracing resemblances between the two poets and the two sides of the coin. The figure implies the complementarity of Yeats and Pound, their high rank among contemporaries, and their continuing value. Metaphorical language can convey complex ideas because it calls on emotional and sensory associations; it is not confined to rational argument. Just because of this, however, it is often inexact:

Do you think I button at the back?

We are a very happening programme and want to be at the cutting edge of any grass.

Figures need to be used with care, so that they elicit the associations you have in mind.

Metaphor and its sibling *simile* (distinguished by its explicit comparison words such as *like* and *as*) are both thought of as composed of *tenor* and *vehicle*. In simile, the tenor (the main thing) and the vehicle (what the main thing is like) are quite distinct:

He may have caught a glimpse of a simile, and it may have vanished again: let him be on the watch for it, as the idle boy watches for the lurking place of the adder.
(Hazlitt, 'On the Difference Between Writing and Speaking')

Here 'let him be on the watch for it' is the tenor while 'as the idle boy watches for the lurking place of the adder' (introduced by the comparison word *as*) is the vehicle. The vehicle often contains a sensory image. It may stay within the figurative discourse altogether, or else have certain shared words in common with the tenor discourse (*watch; watches*). In metaphor, on the contrary, tenor and vehicle parts coalesce, so that the main statement is not literally true:

(1) Teachers are like candles that light others in consuming themselves. (SIMILE)
(2) Teachers are candles lighting others in consuming themselves. (METAPHOR)
(3) The self-consuming candles they learned from. (METAPHOR)

Metaphor is stronger but less obvious; not every reader would understand that (3) refers to teachers.

Figurative language should be used sparingly; it often complicates matters unnecessarily. In literary criticism, indeed, metaphor is usually best avoided altogether; literature itself provides all the figures you need. If your author's metaphors become mixed with your own, it can be hopelessly confusing for the reader. Elusive qualities, however, are sometimes best suggested through metaphor. Hazlitt writes that Coleridge in his talk *appeared to float in air, to slide on ice*. So, too, in the same author's extended contrast between Coleridge and a well-known parliamentarian:

The ideas of the one are as formal and tangible as those

of the other are shadowy and evanescent. Sir James
Mackintosh walks over the ground, Mr. Coleridge is
always flying off from it. The first knows all that has
been said on a subject; the last has something to say
that was never said before.

(Hazlitt, *The Spirit of the Age*)

It would take a great deal of tenor language to say all that
is conveyed in these few figurative sentences.

In close, discursive argument, metaphors are especially
valuable: they alleviate philosophy's dryness and by familiar images give relief from the difficulty of abstraction. Or
their pleasant light may suggest an alternative route to
the conclusion. Francis Bacon often uses such explanatory
images:

> when you carry the light into one corner, you darken
> the rest: so that the fable and fiction of Scylla seemeth
> to be a lively image of this kind of philosophy or
> knowledge; which was transformed into a comely
> virgin for the upper parts; but then . . . there were
> barking monsters all about her loins . . . so the
> generalities of the schoolmen are for a while good and
> proportionable; but then when you descend into their
> distinctions and decisions . . . they end in monstrous
> altercations and barking questions.

(Bacon, *The Advancement of Learning*)

Such applications of metaphor are often developed at
length, and may modulate into metonymy or analogy:

> as water will not ascend higher than the level of the first
> spring-head from whence it descendeth, so knowledge

derived from Aristotle, and exempted from liberty of examination, will not rise again higher than the knowledge of Aristotle.

(The Advancement of Learning)

Here the argument seems unanswerable, the vehicle is so natural: there is no arguing with nature.

Of course figurative language as rich as this would be out of place in ordinary workaday prose. But having such possibilities in mind may help you put together coherent arguments at some length while maintaining readability.

Even the most perfunctory figure should be checked for aptness: the vehicle should suit its tenor—and the tenor's context. In Henry James's 'The Coxon Fund' Mrs Mulville reports the gushing words to her of Miss Anvoy, as Frank Saltram gets into the carriage; her words

> somehow brushed up a picture of Saltram's big shawled back as he hoisted himself into the green landau.

The metaphor *brushed up* (instead of *called up*, say, or *evoked*) is obviously thematic, in that a picture can be painted with a brush; although Saltram's coat may well have needed brushing in another sense. Here the multiple appropriateness lets James get away with a dangerously mixed metaphor—the blurring together of paintbrush and cleaning brush. In general it is best to avoid mixed metaphors, even when they seem safely dead. They have a way of coming alive again; as with the ill-chosen verb *inching*, in 'The public is inching towards the use of kilometres.'

Mixed metaphors are common in official pronouncements:

If we don't grasp the nettle, we risk being left at the roadside, having to get off the economic success shuttle a few years down the line.

Either officials find all metaphors transparent, or they are ambitious to construct extended Baconian figures, without seeing the need for consistency.

It is often said there is no set routine for discovering metaphors. This may be true; but there are regular enough ways of manufacturing them. You begin with the parts or qualities or associations of the tenor thing, and look for metaphors for these. Or you find a simile and strengthen it into metaphor. For example, suppose the thing you want a metaphor for is *reputation*. Simply look it up in a dictionary of quotations (or the Chadwyck-Healy *English Poetry Database* or Wilstach's *Dictionary of Similes*), and you get name, good name, etc., compared to curded milk, glass, precious ointment, a perfectly fitting garment, or jewels— 'Names like jewels flashing the night of time'. If the thing to be figured is *noble sentiment*, the dictionaries will lead you to a simile:

> like gossamer gauze, beautiful and cheap, which will stand no wear and tear.

Then, if you want, you can strengthen the comparison into metaphor:

> sentiment's beautiful gossamer gauze costs little but seldom lasts.

Another source of metaphor is dictionaries of idioms, which as we have seen are often dead metaphors, easily enlivened.

18. Performance and Concurrence

For giving pleasure to the reader, several means are available: you can be lifelike, surprising, witty. But two ways of pleasing stand out, which are commonly neglected: *concurrence*, or multiple expression simultaneously, and *performance*, or enactment of meaning rather than merely stating it. Both are common devices, used in many jokes, like the one about a customer who says to the bookseller 'I want a book about chutzpah—and you're paying.'

The great master of appropriate form is Henry James, who makes sure that the figure in the carpet appears in every piece of the carpet: 'Everything at Poynton was in the style of Poynton.' The urge to perform affects his structure, choice of words, everything. Not content to introduce a speech with 'she said', for example, James individualizes the formula, making it enact his meaning: 'she broke out'; 'she retorted'; 'Miss Overmore continued extremely remote'. Syntax, too, gets in on the act:

> She was wholly powerless to say what Owen would do when he heard of it. 'I don't know what he won't make of you and how he won't hug you!' she had to content herself with lamely declaring.
>
> (James, *The Spoils of Poynton*, ch. 18)

Here the repeated double negatives mime Fleda's conflicted state of mind and failing assurance of Owen's love. Similarly, under Mrs Gereth's pressure, 'Fleda recognised that there was nothing but to hold one's self and bear up'—instead of the idiomatic 'there was nothing for it but to hold' or 'nothing to do but to hold'. Omitting the expected words *for it* or *to do* underlines the absence of any choice at all for Fleda. Joyce Carol Oates uses much the same device when she writes 'In families there are frequently matters of which no one speaks, nor even alludes'. Here, omitting the usual preposition after *alludes* ('matters ... no one alludes to') performs the families' reticence.

Such subtle effects would be out of place in ordinary non-fiction. Still, you may occasionally try to give your reader the pleasure of forms that enact your meaning; you can at least adjust your words to keep in step with the content. Think into language: think of the shape or feel of what you mean, and try for something similar in the words themselves. If you wish to describe an abrupt, staccato movement, for example, it won't do to use smooth, *legato* phrases. If the topic is multifarious, try perhaps for lists, or multiple qualifications.

The fast movement of phrases connected by *and* suits one mood; complex syntax—obliging your reader to construe embedded word groups—goes with quite another, more detached mood. To suggest an intractable problem you might simulate the complication of vicious circles:

To relieve congestion we widen roads or make new ones, which hold out prospects of faster travel, which attracts more vehicles on to the roads—which in turn increases the congestion further. But impasse can be avoided if we only . . .

Here, the syntax goes round and about like the thinking of perplexed planners.

Or suppose you have to contrast two writers, one impressive but ponderous and the other a light, slender talent. You might choose Johnsonian parallelisms for the first, passive constructions for the other:

X's great strength and unflinching steadfastness of purpose contrast with Y's acquiescence in being diverted by every whim.

Again, if you need to suggest sullen, wild, affected behaviour, foreign to ordinary expectations, one way might be to introduce a word that performs this by seeming itself slightly exotic:

Of all the members of the commission, the farouche de Witt stands out.

This requires care, though: the word must not be so unusual as to seem obscure.

Readers will also enjoy it if you introduce *concurrence*—doing several things at once—so that they take in your meaning quicker than they expected. Think how much is going on in Dr Johnson's account of planning his *Dictionary*:

When I took the first survey of my undertaking, I found our speech copious without order, and energetic without rules: wherever I turned my view, there was perplexity to be disentangled, and confusion to be regulated; choice was to be made out of boundless variety, without any established principle of selection; adulterations were to be detected without a settled test of purity; and modes of expression to be rejected or received, without the suffrages [support] of any writers of classical reputation or acknowledged authority.

(Preface, *A Dictionary of the English Language*, 1755)

Everyone notices here the ponderous parallelisms and isocolon (word groups of equal length and structure): 'copious without order . . . energetic without rules'. These not only establish a rhythm but suggest the order Johnson found lacking in previous lexicography. Again, *classical reputation* is close enough to *acknowledged authority* to amount to restatement, while hinting at a distinction between literary models and critical authority. Throughout the sentence Johnson opposes the lexicographer's art to the natural, disorderly state of the language: on this side copiousness, energy, perplexity, confusion, chaotic variety, and adulteration; on that, the application of principles—regulation, selection, ordering, accepting the pure expressions and rejecting the others. By the length of the sentence he amplifies the magnitude of the lonely, many-sided task. And throughout he stresses his total lack of both predecessors and allies by repeating, again and again, the word 'without'. Speech is 'without order'; 'without rules'; he must perform his task 'without an established principle of selection'; 'without a . . . test of purity' and 'without acknowledged authority'. He is on his own, and has to invent the art, thinking it out for himself.

In this giant sentence, Johnson keeps several operations going simultaneously. First, he enumerates tasks: disentangling 'perplexity' (intricate confusion); 'regulating confusion' (discovering the laws of language); selecting from among various forms or spellings of a word; detecting 'adulterations'; and accepting or rejecting 'modes of expression'. Second, he emphasizes how little support he had from authority, particularly since the criteria of ancient literary criticism could not be brought to bear. Third, the form of his intricate syntax, finding its way through many complications, simulates the formidable difficulties before him. So readers quickly share a conspective view of Johnson's huge enterprise, as he reviews it all in a single sentence after the passage of years.

Without attempting prose patterned like Johnson's you can still give your meaning multiple expressions at the same time. Suppose you wish to write about how some administrators inappropriately try to transform the institutions they manage into businesses, forcing their staff to become bean counters. You might begin,

> Financial managers modify each organization they take control of. All they know is money, so they do not make the organization any more efficient, only more profitable financially. The staff they manage have to become amateur accountants.

This is clear enough, but might be more effective if the arguments were made simultaneously:

> → Financial managers do more than manage an organization; they create job descriptions in their own

image, making their staff accountants. Instead of proposals to improve efficiency, staff now make 'bids' and illusory financial projections.

Or take the opening paragraph of a report:

I have considered the proposal with interest. It seemed sincere and helpful. But it originated from one of the most manipulative members of the committee, so I was a bit suspicious. What potential disadvantages did it conceal? First . . .

With concurrence you might put this more concisely, conflating the topic sentence with those that follow:

I have considered this seemingly helpful proposal somewhat suspiciously, knowing its source . . .

In composing paragraphs, you can often combine the various structural functions, accomplishing them simultaneously. The opening paragraph of Nicholson Baker's essay 'Overseas Disposal', for example, sets out the topic under the guise of narration and description:

The British Library's newspaper collection occupies several buildings in Colindale, north of London, near a former Royal Air Force base that is now a museum of aviation. On October 20, 1940, a German airplane— possibly mistaking the library complex for an aircraft-manufacturing plant—dropped a bomb on it. Ten thousand volumes of Irish and English papers were destroyed; fifteen thousand more were damaged. Unscathed, however, was a very large foreign-newspaper collection, including many American titles:

thousands of fifteen-pound brick-thick folios bound in marbled boards, their pages stamped in red with the British Museum's crown-and-lion symbol of curatorial responsibility.

The narration of bombing conveys how vulnerable a library is, at the same time as it establishes the topic, 'The British Library's newspaper collection'; and the description of folios in the foreign-newspaper collection with 'their pages stamped in red with the British Museum's crown-and-lion symbol' provides a visual image, simultaneously with a statement of the library's 'responsibility' for the collection.

Never be content with a single pattern and function: always try to do more. If you have a progression pattern, for example, see if it could usefully be balanced against another, thus reinforcing a comparison. Or if the paragraph structure is one of similar sentences, try perhaps to vary it with alternating sentences in contrast.

19. Revising

Many people who don't write well have simply not revised enough. Students, for example: many students could improve their grades by revising their essays yet have a great reluctance to do so. This may be due to an impatient desire to finish with the task and move on. Or it may come from a sense of failure—the piece is no good and they want nothing more to do with it. Such feelings should be resisted.

Revision need never stop; every time you reread a piece and see possible improvements, you should probably make them. Most writers should keep revising until the deadline is about to be crossed. Revising can go too far: polish can be taken so far that the result is over-refined and lacking in energy. It's a matter of judgement, of course. But excessive revision is rarer than hen's teeth with gold fillings.

Each time you read a draft, look for ways to better it. Local corrections can be made at once, to eliminate inconsistencies, unnecessary words, unnecessary repetitions, grammatical errors, or wooden diction. Other faults, such as ambiguity, buzzwords, favourite jargon, and pointlessly inconsistent registers (different degrees of informality) may be more deep-seated and need extensive rewriting.

Certain improvements are needed so often that with experience they become routine; you can almost make them on autopilot. Wrong pronoun cases, for example, should be obvious enough (although they are becoming less so):

> She gave it to he and I. → She gave it to him and me.
>
> She gave it to him and I. → She gave it to him and me.
>
> Students whom, she conjectured, were exercised by the 'desire to shape poetry into an acceptable product' . . .
> → Students who, she conjectured, were exercised by the 'desire to shape poetry into an acceptable product' . . .

If you are uncertain about pronoun cases, try saying over by themselves the phrases they occur in: *to I; from she; she told he*. Can these be right in standard written English? If you still can't make up your mind it may be time to learn some grammar (see FURTHER READING). Similarly with concord of number, whereby a verb and its subject must agree, both singular or both plural.

> He think → He thinks
>
> They thinks → They think
>
> The Prime Minister and the Cabinet acts as if we had presidential government.
> → The Prime Minister and the Cabinet act as if we had presidential government.

Logical consistency, too, has to be checked:

> Roseanna has been stitched up like a kipper.
>
> There is only one party in this coalition.

Stress has become a four-letter word.

Stock up and save. Limit: one.

Man, honest, will take anything.

Illiterate? Write today for free help.

Entitlement cards will not be compulsory, but everyone will have to have one.

Although the last sentence seems total nonsense, revision might make sense of it. The writer may mean that cards will not be legally required but are likely to prove indispensable in practice.

Rhetorical inconsistencies can be less obvious to the revising eye, and may need more attention. For example, a consistent level of formality should be maintained. If you have already used forms like *you'd think*, it will not do to switch to *one might suppose that* in the next sentence. You should also eliminate needless repetitions of words or sounds, tasteless rhythmic jingles, and similar awkwardnesses:

Walter falters → Walter stumbles.

Meanwhile, while waiting for a response . . .
→ In the interval, while waiting for a response . . .

Equally automatic should be pruning of redundant words, as in

the *hoi polloi* → *hoi polloi* [since *hoi* is itself Greek for 'the']

LCD display → LCD

needless and redundant → needless

theoretically possible → possible

collect together → collect

working dialogue → dialogue

delegate responsibility → delegate

the end result → the result

But such *pleonasm*, or redundancy, is sometimes less obvious:

The World Cup . . . a truly international event

Construction work is rapidly moving apace

Free gift

Naturally such redundancies occur frequently in a working draft; but on rereading (especially aloud) they usually stand out and can easily be eliminated, if necessary with the help of a synonym dictionary. Alternatively, suspected repetitions can be located on-screen by global search. (By keeping a note of the synonyms you substitute, you can avoid new repetitions.) Similarly with unwanted alliteration; except that this is sometimes harder to get rid of. Particularly common are repeated endings in-*ing*:

turning to another engaging thing, affecting every reader . . .

To break up such patterns, the entire syntactic structure may have to be changed:

→ to consider another engaging feature, and one that affects every reader . . .

Such revision is time-consuming but necessary for your reader's pleasure.

One of the most useful improvements you can make is to eliminate deadwood, or inert language. Deadwood not only wastes words to little purpose but also excludes livelier expressions that would communicate more effectively.

through all the stages of implementation → throughout

on the basis of → by

as a consequence of the fact that → because

due to the fact that → because

to such an extent that → so that

in the event that → if

is capable of being → can be

at such a time as → when

on a daily basis → daily

on an occasional basis → occasionally

Often a simple preposition or conjunction can be substituted for a flabby phrase:

for the purpose of → to

of the nature of → like

Some words and phrases are so meaningless that it is best to avoid them wherever possible: for example *fundamentally, essentially, basically, the fact of the matter, in actual fact*. In politicians' speeches, these empty words may serve to gain time while they think on their feet; in writing the deadwood has no function at all.

Basically, I see myself as a frank individual.

(Saul Bellow)

These engines were basically aluminium capsules
with a clip-on nozzle that could be removed in order
to slide in the . . . fuel.   (James Hamilton-Paterson)

Would deleting 'basically' here make any difference?

Official replies to complaints are sometimes so euphem-
istic as to say almost nothing:

Thank you for taking the time to share your
disappointment about the service you have received
from Baggers, your comments are important to us.

(Even the punctuation is incompetent.) Such non-
communication is liable to arouse more fury than a simple
obscenity.

Much unnecessary verbiage can be identified as cliché.
'The net result' often means no more than 'the result'.
Both 'in this day and age' ('nowadays') and 'at this point in
time' ('now') are especially prevalent. Playing one cliché
against the other to keep awake at a committee meeting, I
have known scores as high as 40 : 41. In writing, such
clichés are obviously taboo unless used ironically. Ideally
all the woolly circumlocutions of officialdom should be
sheared off; but a multitude of official communications
have so conditioned us that it is hard now to recognize all
the needless phrases for what they are. In 1913 Quiller-
Couch dismissed as jargon 'in these respects' and 'in the
case of'; now we are inured to both. In fact cliché is the
staple of modern idiomatic language; it could not be eliminated without risking unreal purity. Where would our

headline writers be, without clichés to finesse on? Martin Amis oversimplifies the matter when he pretends to fight a *War Against Cliché*.

Formulas such as 'the bottom line' are phrases overused because they are convenient. By all means try to avoid them; but this won't always be possible. If you use a cliché or idiom (and you often will), you will have to be sure to get it right. False variations creep in, through malapropism:

off his own back → off his own bat

Aide blows the lid → Aide blows the gaffe

Aide drops the beans → Aide spills the beans

muddle the waters → muddy the waters

put a dampener on something → put a damper on something.

Deliberate variation to avoid cliché sometimes makes things worse, as in *the tip of the scandal*. Idioms and formulas should normally be given in full, or they may become meaningless:

Due to circumstances, this shop will be closed on Tuesday.

Here 'circumstances' by itself means too little to make sense. Sometimes, though, careless omission of words results in too much sense, in the shape of an unintended ambiguity:

Five years ago I first used a bar of your soap and since have used no other.

→ Five years ago I first used a bar of your soap and since have used no other brand.

Professional jargon is always moribund. Of course each profession, each science, has a legitimate need for its own specialized vocabulary. But soon jargon comes to be used as a convenient cover for laziness of thought or even (one suspects) obfuscation. The sociological variety of cant deals in inert tropes and cumbrous generalities such as

A system that is tailored to and by the individual and community
→ A system that suits everyone.

Or it will go in for verbs made from nouns by adding -ize: *prioritize; minoritize; conceptualize*; etc.—even *ruggedize*. Business jargon uses fashionable words such as *generate*, as in 'resources must be used to generate income' (for 'make money'). It falls into a linguistic inflation through overuse of such words as *major; massive; significant; critical; relevant*; and *initiative* (instead of *plan* or *programme*). Literary-critical cant prefers vague hypostases: *ethnicity, hegemony, empowerment, patriarchalism*. Translated into ordinary language, such expressions would be too obviously loaded to pass. The jargon of post-structuralist criticism fails even to seem persuasive:

Recuperative ploys such as this are symptomatic of a tendency which would negotiate away those contradictions which constitute the 'factual reality' of the play, reducing drastically its complex discursive structures, smoothing over its complex web of

> contested significations, in the interests of locating
> some controlling idea secreted at its core but anterior
> to its structure—in short, its 'transcendental signified'.
>   (John Drakakis, *Post-structuralist Readings*)

Ideological obscurity is not confined, however, to obvious jargon: it can extend to little words, as when an argument depends on illusory distinctions between prepositions: 'There is hence not repetition and difference, but repetition in difference' (Lacan). Jargon is characterized by routine abstraction; given enough abstractions, a theorist can prove almost anything:

> The opposition between nakedness and being clothed,
> is, of course, a dichotomy similar to the constitutive
> difference between slave and master.
>   (Maureen Quilligan, *Subject and Object*)

Of course it is.

Clarity may seem just a matter of simply writing what you mean. But what you think clear may not seem so to the reader. So a necessary procedure is to read the piece through, imagining at each point what readers' responses are likely to be—the responses especially of enemies. Dr Drall, say, who is and is not a deconstructionist, or Professor Frauenrechtler, a doctrinaire feminist. These imaginary readers lie in ambush, waiting to catch you out. Have you left a signifier floating ambiguously for Drall to seize on? Or a gap in your argument? How might Frauenrechtler misread this masculine pronoun as sexist? Close off every false interpretation a reader could make, watching out for unconsidered stereotypes, male, female, or queer. It isn't enough to be clear: you need to be clear to those determined to misunderstand.

Quiller-Couch used to say 'write masculine English'—choosing active verbs and concrete nouns in preference to abstract and 'foggy wording'. But of course qualities of writing can't be attributed to a single gender: think of Jane Austen's strength, or George Eliot's, or Angela Carter's. And if Frauenrechtler jeers at my praising women writers for power and strength and penetration I shall hold my ground. Quiller-Couch's advice, rightly understood, is not really about gender. Beginning a sentence 'There are those who say that' is usually inferior to 'Some say that', just as active constructions are often better than passives:

> A reference list of all Enterprise Projects and the relevant Project Co-ordinators is enclosed.
> → I enclose a reference list of all Enterprise Projects and related Project Co-ordinators.

All the same, passives can be hard to replace. They are needed, for example, to get over the awkwardness of indefinite agents in English; you may well find it convenient to leave the agent unmentioned, if you have to tell someone 'Your car has been borrowed'. Besides, passives may be desirable for variety, or to express delicate, yielding, constrained, or negative feelings. Similarly with abstract nouns. By all means cut down on them; but concrete nouns will not always serve the turn.

Use short, simple words wherever possible: it saves your reader's time. Prefer short words to long, simple expressions to complicated, pompous ones. Cut down especially on wordy, nominal constructions (syntax based on nouns):

He shows a proneness to impulsivity.
→ He tends to be impulsive.

the constative dimension of that discourse [Hegel's] is thus inseparable from a performative aspect

(Terry Eagleton)

→ that system is inescapably political.

Generally prefer verbal constructions (that is, ones where verbs rather than nouns carry most of the meaning).

Once you have achieved a revised draft, read it through quickly to remind yourself of the sentence structure and rhythm (not just the rhythm of individual phrases but of whole paragraphs), and to spot gross flaws such as undesirable repetitions. If you notice any, don't immediately change to revision mode and introduce improvements. Instead, mark up the printout but keep on reading: you need to get an impression of the overall movement and rhythm. In the course of this scan, watch out for parenthetic notes, which easily interrupt the flow. On the other hand, anything like a regular rhythm is of course undesirable: inadvertent blank verse is a fault, not an accidental felicity. Above all, use this quick scan to detect overloaded sentences.

The next objective might be to break up monotonous routines: never let yourself become predictable. So vary the length of word groups, vary the length of sentences, change every regularity. If a sentence seems very abstract, make the next one restate it in the most concrete possible terms. In lists, it need hardly be said, variation is a mandatory aim.

Notices, advertisements, or testimonials are especially worth checking for possible ambiguity. There are humorists out there, just waiting.

We do not tear your clothing with machinery. We do it carefully by hand.

Used cars. Why go elsewhere to be cheated? Come here first.

Wanted: hair cutter. Excellent growth potential.

Our bikinis are exciting. They are simply the tops.

We will oil your sewing machine and adjust tension in your home.

Auto repair service. Free pickups and delivery. Try us once, you'll never go anywhere else again.

Sometimes, of course, you may prefer to leave an ambiguity as it stands:

Anyone getting this man to work for him will be lucky.

He left us as he came to us, fired with enthusiasm.

Such ambiguities became commoner when testimonials ceased to be confidential.

Unintentional ambiguity often arises from uncertainty about the antecedent—as to what noun a pronoun replaces:

Look out for the brand new Vehicle Registration Certificate arriving in the post between now and June 2005. If you haven't already received one, and you tax your vehicle using the automated renewal reminder form, it'll come shortly afterwards. You will also get one following a Statutory Off Road Notification. When it arrives, please make sure that you destroy your old style log-book. Whatever you do, don't lose it. A replacement will cost you £19.

Why should the old-style log-book be preserved? And what will 'arrive'—the Statutory Off Road Notification, or the reminder form, or the Registration Certificate? Similar confusion arises with

The audience of business leaders, MSPs and academics was told that Edinburgh must co-operate with Glasgow and urgently address its infrastructure problems in order to remain an economically successful European city.

Whose problems is Edinburgh to 'address': Glasgow's or its own? Normally a pronoun stands in for the noun immediately preceding.

Try to keep a balance between emotive and neutral words. Don't rush to an extreme word like *demolish*, for example, if *criticize* will do instead. In areas where offensiveness threatens, it's worth being particularly careful to avoid overstatement, without however limiting yourself to bland conventionalities. Such routine changes as I have mentioned will soon become second nature. Yet, as you make them, others less routine may suggest themselves.

You can use the global search command to detect disproportions of various sorts. A search for *is, been*, etc. may show up too many passives and flabby constructions, and a search for *-tion, -ness*, etc. may expose excessive abstraction or too many nominal constructions.

It helps to have a model of good writing. Or, better, several models. (After all, you wouldn't go to P. G. Wodehouse for the ideal letter of condolence, nor to Henry James for a telegram.) Contemporary writing unfortunately offers few dependable models, and is liable besides to tempt you with fashionable clichés. Yet many canonical authors—think of Conrad, Meredith, or Pater—would hardly be suitable either. In his low-profile way V. S. Naipaul has a fine standard of finish. Kingsley Amis used to favour Wodehouse, despite his being habitually parodistic. For shorter pieces, C. S. Lewis sets a benchmark, and for ambitious expository writing E. H. Gombrich is an excellent model. To achieve natural diction, you could do worse than follow Frank Kermode. For rhythm, you might study the early Ernest Hemingway; or Walter de la Mare; or the King James Bible. In the USA, all the registers are different, but, for various purposes, Lionel Trilling, Eudora Welty, and Anthony Grafton have all produced bodies of writing worth study.

20. Correctness

Writing aims to communicate, not to be correct. In any case one can never be perfectly correct in every respect, for there are many sorts of correctness, according to the readership, the kind of writing, and the variety of language. The requirements of one correctness may not be compatible with those of another. For example the demands of formal precision conflict with the requirements of informality: informal, colloquial language is fine for a private letter or email but won't do for a learned journal. Conventions of political correctness may have to be followed in an official report, even if they militate against the requirements of good prose. Again, words that are quite intelligible to one age-group may be obscure double-talk to another. No one knows more than a small part of their language, so it's no disgrace to be vague about some of the grammar. Anyhow, 'correct English is the slang of prigs', as George Eliot said.

Grammatical correctness is no simple matter of obeying a single set of agreed rules. Spoken language is often 'incorrect'; if you choose to write informally ('like you speak') you have to use forms you know break the strictest rules. In written language, on the other hand, gross solecisms must be avoided. In a scale of errors wrong pronoun cases count as pretty heinous, yet they occur in speech and in literary works such as Pepys's *Diary*. In the very long term, case distinctions may be on the way out. A modern critic writes

> some bright spark in Teleland decided that it was much too strange to be enjoyed by we idiot viewers.
> → some bright spark in Teleland decided that it was much too strange to be enjoyed by us idiot viewers.

And a newspaper columnist provides a similar example:

> for both he and General Clark, that may be the realistic peak of their ambition.
> → for both him and General Clark, that may be the realistic peak of their ambition.

Did these journalists consciously decide against the correct forms, *by us* and *for . . . him*?

A less heinous error is the use of *like* as a conjunction:

> The . . . pyramid-spires of Bosch's Bethlehem look like they came off the cover of a 1970s Asimov paperback.
> → The . . . pyramid-spires of Bosch's Bethlehem look as if they came off the cover of a 1970s Asimov paperback.

Here many would consider *look as if* more correct. But the ugly, informal *like*, which has been around for centuries, is gaining ground.

Then, there are errors that have been recategorized as correct—perhaps too enthusiastically. It used to be thought wrong to split an infinitive, for example by inserting an adverb: *to casually remark*. But then realistic grammarians, such as Robert Burchfield (editing *Fowler's Modern English Usage*, 1996) conceded 'that rigid adherence to a policy of non-splitting can sometimes lead to unnaturalness or ambiguity'. We were free to split when it sounded better to do so. Which was fine. But now (it had to happen) the permissive policy of Burchfield has hardened into a rule. Many writers go out of their way to split infinitives even when the effect is awkward: *to boldly go*.

Another error is identified by the jurist Geoffrey Marshall as 'the sportsman's conditional':

> If Arsenal had pressed harder in the second half they may have won.
> → If Arsenal had pressed harder in the second half they might have won.

> Had Venables stayed, he may have been good enough to get England through.
> → Had Venables stayed, he might have been good enough to get England through.

But it may be wrong to single out the sports journalists. More likely the 'error' is due to a changing use of modal verbs in hypothetical sentences. The distinction between *may* and *might* to indicate real versus unreal possibilities is becoming less clear-cut. The fatalistic will see such changes as irreversible trends. Even so, they are trends one can choose either to resist or to accelerate. Do we really want to lose the distinction between real and unreal hypotheses?

Accepting certain errors may be regarded as a matter of deciding how precise you want to be.

> None of them were present.

> None of them was present.

Each of these sentences is correct in certain contexts. *None* is not a short form of *no one*, but derives from Old

English *nan*: its use with a plural verb has always been optional:

> though she had many affairs, none were lighthearted
> romances.   (*New Yorker*, 1987)

Use the singular verb where you can, particularly if you aim for strict correctness. But the plural verb may be preferable if the context has a strongly plural sense.

As we saw in the last chapter, *unique* (unequalled) is not gradable: a thing either is unique or not; *very unique* is a solecism. Colloquial use to mean 'unusual', however, is now so common that the original meaning may be weakening. All the same it is still worth defending; *most unique* is out of place, for example, in an academic journal:

> One of America's oldest literary genres and its most
> unique . . .
> → One of America's oldest literary genres and its most
> distinctive . . .

Education in the UK has declined so far that lexical errors (wrong word choices) are now quite frequent:

> abrogating *for* arrogating, *as in* abrogating to
> themselves the right
> palette *for* palate, *as in* tailored to the American palate
> reticent *for* reluctant, *as in* reticent to sell supplies to
> the society
> secluded *for* excluded, *as in* I just feel really secluded
> quaffed *for* coiffed, *as in* quaffed hair
> wreckless *for* reckless, *as in* much of our litter is simply
> the result of wreckless actions

consequentially *for* consequently, *as in* his voice was new and, consequentially, striking

conspire *for* confer, *as in* the defence requests a recess so that I may conspire with my client

dictat *for* dictum, *as in* there is that dictat the old ones are the best

beggar *for* augur, *as in* it does not beggar well

herald *for* hail, *as in* whose family herald from Fife.

All these examples are from current periodicals or political speeches. In such contexts a wrongly chosen word may even mean the opposite of what is intended, as in

the approbation she faced from her strait-laced society . . .

there are many ingenuous [= clever] design elements.

The last example has a déjà vu feel, for it reverses the seventeenth-century error that gave us our present senses of the two words *ingenious* and *ingenuous*.

From lexical errors ambiguity often results; as with *the sight/site of the castle.* 'Whatever. It's only a word.' Pairs of words prone to confusion include

acceptance *and* acceptation
affect *and* effect
alternate *and* alternative
ambiguous *and* ambivalent
baleful *and* baneful
ceremonial *and* ceremonious
complementary *and* complimentary
compose *and* comprise

contemptible *and* contemptuous
convince *and* persuade
deprecate *and* depreciate
derisive (contemptuous) *and* derisory (inadequate)
discreet *and* discrete
disinterested *and* uninterested
forceful *and* forcible
imply *and* infer
judicious *and* judicial
luxuriant *and* luxurious
manically *and* maniacally
masterful *and* masterly
perspicacity *and* perspicuity
purport *and* purpose
reversal *and* reversion
seasonal *and* seasonable
sensuous *and* sensual
triumphal *and* triumphant
unexceptional *and* unexceptionable

Each of these words may be worth looking up in a modern dictionary before you use it. Kingsley Amis described the longer list in *Fowler's Modern English Usage* as inflated for show, but he is proved wrong by the increasing imprecision of language. How are we to arrest the decline? Although such books as Amis's may help, there is only one way for writers to avoid lexical errors: to consult good dictionaries more often. Don't rely on a spellchecker or electronic thesaurus for this; it will supply the wrong word as soon as the right one. So never write further away from a dictionary than the length of the arm you're chancing.

Especially for a journalist, lexical errors are insulting to the reader.

Of course, lexical errors can also be delicious sometimes, perhaps deliberately so. *Preprolapsian* for *prelapsarian* was an innocent error, and *antiquititious* for *antique*. But such words as *volumptuous* (from *voluptuous* and *sumptuous*) may be more calculated.

Many British people find it amusing sometimes to write American, using words and idioms and catch phrases such as *way* (= far) as in 'way in excess' (Catherine Belsey); *no way* (= certainly not); *way to go*; or *that's the name of the game*. In speech there is nothing wrong with borrowing from other varieties of English, perhaps for jocular effect. Or from other languages: 'Is it that you have the intention to not miss the train?' In the case of writing, however, American English borrowings need to be consciously considered if they are not to produce uncertainties of meaning:

I don't care to walk it.

(Barbara Kingsolver, *Prodigal Summer*).

Does this mean 'I don't mind walking it' or 'I don't wish to walk it'? On the other hand, apparent borrowings sometimes turn out to have long indigenous pedigrees: for example, *no way* ('certainly not') has been a British English usage continually since at least 1787. It is much the same with British English borrowings in the USA; although nowadays American English, thanks to its rich creativity, tends to be more of an exporter of usages.

Many words and idioms differ between British and American varieties of English:

British	American
behind; at the back of	in back of
oversleep	sleep in
blow your own trumpet	blow your own horn
cap in hand	hat in hand

Writers should at least try to be aware when they are writing American English and when British.

In politics, ignorance and jargon interact to bring about a special type of passionate incoherence:

> highly sub-optimal

> We need to upskill Scotland from the bottom down.

> Things are more like they are now than they have ever been.

Both political discourse and job descriptions often contain euphemisms and inflated circumlocutions using the jargon of salesmanship. Phrases such as *twilight merchandiser* and *ambient replenishment operative* may be in line with contracts of employment, but they are too obscure for good writing.

Errors also arise in pursuing political correctness. The PC convention aims to avoid giving offence, especially in the media and the workplace. With this in mind, managers reasonably forbid the use of words objectionable to racial or ethnic minorities (blacks, Roman Catholics, Jews, and others) as well as one majority group, women. It's surely reasonable to avoid offensive words such as *nigger, pape, yid, cow*. The trouble is that PC doesn't stop there, but extends to all words that could conceivably cause offence. These are proscribed and listed together with inoffensive, temporarily acceptable alternatives in sizeable dictionaries. For example, any word must be avoided that could imply an ancillary role for women: *waitress, actress*, etc. Instead, asexual designations like *waitron* are proposed; and *wimmin* or *wymmyn* replaces *women* (*wo-men*) for those who repudiate men altogether. But such usages (*herstory* for *history* is another) fail to engage with language in a serious way: it can't be altered lastingly at the behest of individuals. Unfortunately those most interested in changing the language are also those least interested in etymology. So *niggardly* (grudging) is condemned because of an imagined association with *nigger*.

A problem arises with the indefinitely gendered pronoun *he* (*his*, etc.). This is commonly solved by resorting to *he or she*, a cumbrous formulation that can break almost any sentence's rhythm. Another solution, worse because confusingly ambiguous, is to alternate *he* and *she*, leaving the reader to puzzle out whether the antecedent has changed in reality, or only in gesture. Such devices go for the quick fix of a superficial linguistic correctness, without considering the consequences. It is far better to restructure the syntax, if you can, so that the problem doesn't arise. But if you get stuck, you can always have recourse to *they*: better to break grammatical concord than social accord. (The form *themself* was used by Caxton, as early as 1489.)

The PC movement has given rise to many euphemisms for social groups that need none: *handicapable* (handicapped); *differently able* (disabled); *physically challenged* (handicapped); *differently hirsute* (bald); *person of colour* (non-white); *experientially challenged* (old); *person of substance* (obese person); etc. For PC goes in for generalizing abstractions, as when the idiomatic *coloured man* becomes *a man of colour* or *a person of colour*. Such language can be unhelpfully vague. Is the *person of colour* male or female? Which *special needs* are meant? Does an *abuse* refer to rape or excessive punishment? Further definition, legal or clinical, is likely to be needed.

Again, if you are never to refer to anyone in negative terms you will tend to write obscurely: *non-traditional shopper* doesn't immediately convey 'shoplifter'. Such obscurities proliferate, since managers are apprehensive about litigation, while affirmative action officers naturally wish to extend their territory by exploring unobvious, theoretically imaginable causes of offence. When *black* was rejected as a term for negro, *black sheep* was also proscribed as somehow racist. *Able-bodied* must be replaced by *person who is non-disabled*; and *a schizophrenic* by *a person who has schizophrenia*.

Especially in local government and social services, an insensitive version of PC may be thought to have made excessive inroads, with counterproductive consequences. First, it gives managers pretexts for misuse of power. A Washington official notoriously lost his job for using the innocent word *niggardly* at a staff meeting. It may seem ludicrous that any manager should suppose *niggardly* derives from *nigger* or even *niger*; but the man who lost his job was not laughing—nor perhaps were the blacks who felt patronized. Another consequence of thoughtless PC is that it diverts attention from actions to words.

Instead of pressing for reform of discriminatory practices it offers a war of words about theoretical slights. Elaborate restrictions on vocabulary hinder communication just where it needs to be most effective. Replacing *discussion* by *dialogue* or *sharing* does nothing to promote real exchanges of views. Similarly, the very classics (such as *Little Black Sambo*) that might help to bridge cultural divides are banned from libraries and schools for PC reasons.

In writing for mixed readerships, you will obviously have to consider carefully which words might be painful to others; be alert for both real and imagined slights. If you are a man writing for women (or vice versa) you need to be aware of expectations of sexism. You may think it advisable to consult a dictionary of PC forms (see REFERENCE BOOKS), to heighten your consciousness and exercise your patience.

In revising advanced drafts, keep a lookout for unwanted double meanings. These are always liable to crop up in quotations from older writers, for, as the language changes, readers' associations change too. So watch out for unintended humour, particularly in quotations from serious writers such as Milton ('touched my trembling ears'); William Cowper ('crack the satiric thong'); or Elizabeth Barrett Browning ('panting red pants into the west'). But the danger is ubiquitous. A campaign speech writer has to be careful about mentioning the Titanic: the name's associations evoke disaster. In fact, at the final stage of writing you need to screen every word.

21. Reducing

So, you thought you could ignore everything said about DRAFTS above; you went straight ahead and wrote the piece without giving any thought to scale. Or else vital new material came to hand late on. Or you went into denial and 'forgot' to give the word count command. So now your penultimate draft is far over the word limit, and all that work of composition has turned out to be wasted effort—work spent making occasion for more work. It's no use pretending the excess wordage won't be noticed, no use trying to disguise the extra pages by single spacing or a minute font size. The piece will have to be cut.

Take heart: it's no great disaster. You have two remedies, according to how far you've gone over the limit. First, you can cut paragraphs, quotations, examples, or other entire features. If you are, say, 30 per cent over, this remedy can't be avoided, even if it damages the piece. All you can do to limit the damage is to cut the passages least central to your argument, perhaps substituting a few words to explain that certain topics lie outside your plan. This drastic remedy can give rapid relief if you are ruthless enough.

The second remedy is *reducing*, or boiling down. This keeps the sequence, argument, and proportions intact, but usually can eliminate only about a tenth of the words. Besides, reducing is liable to make the piece less readable. Up to a point, cutting out inessentials—qualifications and details, perhaps—may actually improve the writing; but only up to a point. Beyond that, concision tends to become dry or overabstract. Extremely concise writing can even become difficult or obscure. You don't want to cut so much as to approach telegraphese and ambiguity: 'How old Cary Grant?' will open the door to the reply 'Old Cary Grant fine.'

Vague language requires wordy qualification, so that increasing the precision may reduce verbiage:

People who manage others → Managers.

Often, too, wordiness arises from using nouns (occasionally verbs) where a simple adjective or adverb would be briefer. Ask yourself, can I put this more succinctly using another part of speech?

He indicated his preference for thrillers with plenty of action.
→ He said he preferred action thrillers.

Similarly with overuse of the verb *to be* (easily detected by global searches):

There is a tendency for social reformers to lose their sense of responsibility for the underprivileged as soon as there is an increase in their own salaries.
→ When social reformers earn more they tend to feel less responsible for the underprivileged.

Circumlocutions for *because* or other simple conjunctions seldom earn their keep: you can eradicate them without remorse:

The reform failed as a consequence of the fact that many of the reformers were half-hearted.

→ The reform failed because many of the reformers were half-hearted.

You may also be able to reduce the word count by tightening up sentence structures. Sometimes a single word can replace an entire phrase with little if any loss:

She spoke in a pretentious manner. → She spoke pretentiously.

Or a mere punctuation point may do much of the work of a phrase or clause:

The Renaissance had several causes, which may be summarized as improvements in education and the recovery of ancient culture, together with the spread of ideas through printing.

→ The Renaissance had several causes: improvements in education, recovery of ancient culture, and spread of ideas through printing.

Simple constructions are generally briefer than complex ones:

When he had come to the country, he explored it until he had a good idea of the strength of the enemy; then he was in a position to defeat them.

→ He came; he saw; he conquered.

Active constructions usually need fewer words than passive ones:

He was defeated by the Iceni. → The Iceni defeated him.

Here changing to the active voice saves two of the six words.

In parallel constructions, a word or two can frequently be omitted without loss of clarity:

> The best candidate for election is not always the best statesman after the election is over.
> → The best candidate for election is not always the best statesman afterwards.

In omitting words from such constructions you can easily go wrong through not sustaining the parallel. You have to sustain it scrupulously. So in reducing

> She did not choose the problem nor did she ever really understand the importance of DNA and its structure.

it will not quite do to substitute the simple past tense:

> She did not choose the problem nor ever really understood the importance of DNA and its structure.

If you want to maintain the construction, the verbs need to be in parallel:

> → She did not choose the problem nor [did she] ever really understand the importance of DNA and its structure.

Here the verbs ('choose'; 'understand') match exactly.

Many writers introduce their opinions with elaborate manoeuvring that can easily be cut; although of course some nuances may be lost:

> It seems very much as if the Renaissance academies were more receptive to new ideas.

→ The Renaissance academies were more receptive to new ideas.

I might not altogether be exaggerating if I were to venture the assertion that Smith is virtually the only serious candidate.

→ Smith is virtually the only serious candidate.

Reducing may sometimes positively improve the piece; as when you cut introductory palavar explaining what you are going to do later on:

I should like to begin by refuting all previous hypotheses about these phenomena. Then I shall proceed to construct a theory giving a complete explanation of them.

Such boasts are unlikely to impress a great many readers. Elaborate announcements, manoeuvring into a correct stance, flying an ideological flag: such rigmaroles put readers off. Just write what you mean:

It is certainly the case that many reports are too long.

→ Many reports are too long.

The looser the style, the easier it is to reduce:

In 1943, by which point Kingsley was a 21-year-old Oxford undergraduate and a lieutenant in the army, William discovered that his son was having an affair with a married woman.   (Martin Amis, *Experience*)

Suppose Martin Amis had decided to reduce this by 25 per cent, it would not have been difficult:

In 1943, when Kingsley was a 21-year-old Oxford

undergraduate and army lieutenant, William
discovered his son was having an adulterous affair.

And the sentence could be reduced still further:

In 1943, when Kingsley was 21, William discovered
his adulterous affair.

Reduction has now removed more than half the words,
through changes that affect the content considerably, losing some information. Be careful in reducing to keep the
most relevant parts and cut inessentials; keep asking
yourself not only 'Is this completely relevant?' but also 'Is
this, after all, indispensable?'

Sometimes you can reduce the word count (and inci-
dentally improve the prose) by making the same phrase
serve multiple functions. A topic sentence, for example,
can simultaneously convey the topic and your view of it.
(See under PERFORMANCE AND CONCURRENCE.)

When you have reduced as much as you need to, go on
and reduce a little more. The aim of this is to allow for
flexibility in later revision. When you draft your final version you may want to add a few words here and there, to
clean up any rough edges the cuts have left—which have a
way of appearing only when you print the piece out and
read it through.

22. Research: Hard and Soft

Sometimes writing proves difficult because you don't know enough: READING and memory may not provide all the material you need. Then it may be necessary to extend your knowledge by research, that is, systematic searching for information and ideas. How is research best begun?

Many people go straight to the Internet: that must be a sound move whenever speed is an important factor. The Internet quickly provides more information than you can easily handle. In fact, if you are working on a short piece, consulting the Internet may be all the research you need do, in the early stages of writing. Current ideas and new words are particularly well covered on the Web: for example, you can hope to find information on nonce expressions, some with their own sites, like 'jumping the shark'. Nevertheless there are limits to what the Internet can do for you.

You soon come up against these limitations even in bibliographic and other databases, among the Internet's chief glories. Not so long ago, tests showed that in compiling a bibliography, you will find on-screen only about a quarter as many items as you could find in books (annual and special area bibliographies, monograph footnotes, etc.). Some computer databases ignore publications before around 1980; others neglect most of those published abroad. Of course this situation is improving all the time; a great advance has come with electronic versions of library catalogues. Another limitation concerns the quality of information retrieved from the Internet. Much of the anonymous information, in particular, is inaccurate, so that, if you are writing a scholarly piece, you may have to rework the research behind the material you find. A third limitation is sheer impermanence: Internet resources have a way of not being there when you next try to use them.

The success of the Internet—the sheer magnitude of its unmanageably copious contents—occasions difficulties of a different sort. Like a cosmic scrapbook it seems to contain everything; except that almost all it contains is irrelevant. Its information is certainly far too voluminous to be easily available: among its billions of pages, how are you to find the one you need? It is a trackless forest where you can easily feel lost; yet it may well hide what you need behind the next tree.

To search the Internet you need a *search engine*. Search engines (dozens of them exist) are huge databases consisting of extracts from the billions of Web 'pages'; when you submit search words, a list of *hits* appears from the pages scanned. Currently, the best engine for many purposes is Google (http://www.google.com), which is likely to confront you, at first, with more hits than you can handle. To use the engine in a discriminating way, you will need the invaluable *Google: The Missing Manual* (Sebastopol, Calif.: O'Reilly, 2004), by Sarah Milstein and Rael Dornfest. You will learn to think of unlikely, exclusively relevant search words. Proper names are good, although you may still find doppelgängers such as *John Smith* the politician and *John Smith* the industrial firm. Conversely,

Google treats different spellings of the same name or word as different words; so you may have to try spelling variants: *John Smith, John C. Smith, John Smyth,* etc.

Other Internet resources include specialized *subject directories, portals,* or *hubs*: sites that direct you to other places to look. For example try Humbul Humanities Hub (www.humbul.ac.uk) or The Voice of the Shuttle (vos.ucsb.edu). These *gateway* or *portal* databases can be more selective than Google; but they are cumbrous to use, and often engage in the sort of search more quickly carried out through books. Their great virtue lies in their classifying structure; and in leading on to a variety of other resources—institutional sites, for example, or electronic texts. Electronic legal databases are particularly useful for their plentiful extracts. Random examples are Infolaw at www.infolaw.co.uk and Lawoffice.com at www.lawoffice.com. Legal search engines such as Westlaw are huge but expensive, effectually limited to institutional use. For Web sites relating to specialized areas of research it is worth consulting Angus J. Kennedy, *The Rough Guide to the Internet* (London: Rough Guides).

Whatever electronic resources you draw on, you eventually arrive at references to books and articles. These you may be able to sample online, or download; generally at this stage you turn to hard copy—to printed-out or printed sources. For you need to read unabridged sources rather than mere extracts. In the end writing comes from reading, rather than consulting screens.

Research methods are the subject of a great many books, between most of which there is not much to choose. They range from elementary introductions, treating library skills and common sense, to specialized contributions on advanced research techniques. Most are American, and have much to say about the preparation of academic theses and the minutiae of footnote styling. Elementary general guides include Nancy L. Baker, *A Research Guide for Undergraduate Students: English and American Literature*, 2nd edn. (New York: Modern Language Association, 1985), and Richard D. Altick, *The Art of Literary Research*, 3rd edn., rev. John J. Fenstermaker (New York: Norton, 1981). Of more advanced treatments, one of the best is James L. Harner, *Literary Research Guide* (New York: Modern Language Association of America, 1989); but older, general works such as Jacques Barzun and Henry F. Graff's *The Modern Researcher*, 4th edn. (San Diego, Calif.: Harcourt, 1985), and Lester A Beaurline (ed.), *A Mirror for Modern Scholars* (New York: Odyssey, 1966) are still valuable, and have much to teach.

One secret of searching is to follow many distinct lines of approach, and switch from one to another whenever you find yourself blocked. Never get bogged down in a slavish task of monotonous searching; there's always a more intelligent way. Pursuing a specialized topic, for example, you could plod through subject bibliographies; but keyword searches are usually quicker, whether in a bibliographic database or an electronic version of a library catalogue. Concordances and dictionaries of quotations, too, often give unexpected help. Or you could try Boolean searches for words and phrases in the electronic *OED*, and (for literary searches) *The English Poetry Database*. Annual bibliographies are safest for systematic searching. But you might find a shortcut through documentation of recent journal articles (a long shot) or footnote citations in books. Indexes to well-edited classics of a miscellaneous nature, such as John Evelyn's *Diary* or Robert Burton's *Anatomy of Melancholy*, sometimes prove unexpectedly rewarding.

Summon all your powers of lateral thinking to broaden the combination search method. You might go from an *OED* quotation to the edition cited, consult the notes or bibliography of a more recent edition of the source, then go on to a journal article referred to in *that* edition; finding there a phrase you hadn't thought of as a possible keyword for a Web search. Or a browsing reconnaissance to size up the problem might prompt a long systematic hunt through a searchable, electronic version of a canonical text.

23. Reference Books

'For a desert island, one would choose a good dictionary rather than the greatest literary masterpiece imaginable' (W. H. Auden). Many love reference books because they lead on from entry to entry in an unexpected way and arrive at marvellous serendipities. Besides, you don't have to read them through.

You can get by with very few reference books on your shelves, so long as you have easy access to a large library or to the Internet. For the latter, Jennifer Rowley's *The Electronic Library*, 4th edn. (London: Facet, 2003), is indispensable.

From time to time you should consult (although not necessarily own) at least one book on how to write. These are so many that any recommendations must be very selective. Robert Graves and Alan Hodge's *The Reader over your Shoulder* (London: Cape, 1943, 1947) used to be the best; it is very dated now, but still worth dipping into. G. H. Vallins, *Good English: How to Write It* (London: Deutsch, 1964) has much grammatical detail, while Richard A. Lanham, *Analyzing Prose*, 2nd edn. (London and New York: Continuum, 2003), focuses on rhetoric. For journalists, Harold Evans's *Newsman's English* is a must. For students (particularly US students), Thomas Kane's *The Oxford Guide to Writing* (1983), with wide coverage and full examples, has much to offer. If you have many short deadlines, you should read Sanford Kaye's *Writing under Pressure* (1989). Peter Elbow's unsystematic essay collection *Everyone Can Write* (2000) contains much excellent advice from a seasoned composition teacher.

One book you should certainly own is a dictionary, to be kept close at hand at all times. For writing, a smallish one is best: the *New Penguin*, say, or the *Concise Oxford* (120,000 entries). If you need more words, consult the two-volume *Shorter Oxford Dictionary* (500,000 definitions; electronic version available), or even the twenty-volume *OED* second edition (also published in compact and electronic versions). Electronic versions of small dictionaries work well. Larger dictionaries are a powerful resource, indispensable for advanced searching; they help to lay the foundation of most long-term research projects. But they are not always easy to consult quickly: if space and expense are not a problem, best have both hard and soft versions (the latter installed on your hard disk rather than on CD-ROM).

You will also need a dictionary of synonyms, so as to review alternative expressions and find the exact word—or simply get you going when your brain is sluggish and can't quite remember that word which would be just right. The most useful sort of thesaurus allows access in one step like an ordinary dictionary: for example Rosalind Fergusson, Martin Manser, and David Pickering, *The Penguin Thesaurus* (2000 and later editions); J. I. Rodale, *The Synonym Finder* (1978 and later editions). Others have an index of topics or of semantic fields, so that getting to the words is a two-stage procedure, as in *Roget's International Thesaurus* (Pearson) or *Roget's Thesaurus* (Collins).

For distinctions between similar words (*as* and *since; nor* and *or*) the most practical resource is a dictionary of usage, such as R. W. Burchfield's *The New Fowler's Modern English Usage* (1996) or Kingsley Amis's challenging *The King's English* (1997). For finicky points of spelling or punctuation, consult *The Oxford Dictionary for Writers and Editors* (2000); Pam Peters, *The Cambridge Guide to English Usage* (2004); or *The Chicago Manual of Style*, 15th edn. Punctuation is fully treated in Eric Partridge, *You Have a Point There* (1953), and more recently in Burchfield and in Lynne Truss's combative *Eats, Shoots and Leaves* (2003).

To prompt your memory of phrases, there are dictionaries of idioms such as John O. E. Clark's *Word Wise* (1988); Daphne M. Gulland and David G. Hinds-Howell's *The Penguin Dictionary of English Idioms* (1986); or T. H. Long and D. Summers's *Longman Dictionary of English Idioms* (1979) (4,500 items). Idiom shades off into proverb and catch-phrase, so you might also consult *The Concise Oxford Dictionary of Proverbs* (1982); *The Oxford Dictionary of English Proverbs*, 3rd edn. (1970); Eric Partridge's *A Dictionary of Catch Phrases* (1977); Martin H. Manser's *Proverbs* (New York: Facts on File, 2002) (1,500 sayings); Elizabeth Knowles's *The Oxford Dictionary of Phrase and Fable* (2000) (20,000 items); or—the grandfather of them all—*Brewer's Dictionary of Phrase and Fable* (London: Cassell, many edns. since 1870). For similes you might find useful Frank J. Wilstach, *A Dictionary of Similes* (rev. edn.: New York: Bonanza, 1924) (nearly 20,000 similes); Hugh Rawson, *A Dictionary of Euphemism and other Double Talk* (1981); or the quotations in a large dictionary.

A number of dictionaries of slang claim attention here: formidable contributions to our understanding of informal language have been made by Eric Partridge, *A Dictionary of Slang and Unconventional English*, 8th edn. (Routledge & Kegan Paul, 1984); Jonathon Green, *Cassell's Dictionary of Slang* (London: Cassell, 2006); Harold Wentworth and Stuart Berg Flexner, *Dictionary of American Slang*, 2nd edn. (New York: Crowell, 1960); Richard A Spears, *NTC's Dictionary of American Slang and Colloquial Expressions* (Lincolnwood, Ill.: National Textbook Company, 1989) (9,000 items); and Jonathan Lighter, *The Random House Historical Dictionary of American Slang* (ongoing). Almost by definition slang dictionaries can never be quite up to date.

A surprising amount of time can go in tracing a half-remembered quotation. Here especially it is vital not to become sidetracked in searching mechanically through a whole work, unless there is no alternative. Use a concordance, when there is one. Or, if you have access to electronic databases, try the Chadwyck-Healy *English Poetry Database*. The chance of scoring a hit in a large database is obviously greater, but the search may take some considerable time. Dictionaries of quotations are quicker, and increasingly are available in electronic versions. If you know the author of a quotation, it may be quicker to consult a dictionary arranged under authors, such as *The Oxford Dictionary of Quotations* (1953 etc.; each edition differs from its predecessor, without noticeable improvement). If you don't remember the author or the text, or want as many quotations as possible on a specific subject, try John Bartlett, *Familiar Quotations* (1955 etc., arranged by topic) or Burton Stevenson's huge *Stevenson's Book of Quotations Classical and Modern* (over 2,816 pages and 70,000 quotations in the 10th edn. of 1974).

The above are general dictionaries; but sometimes specialized ones can be more useful. For literary quotations try Meic Stephens's *A Dictionary of Literary Quotations* (3,250 items, 1990); *The Oxford Dictionary of Literary Quotations* (4,400 items, 1997); or, best of all, David Crystal and Hilary Crystal's *Words on Words: Quotations about Language and Languages* (London: Penguin, 2000) (5,000 items). Modern quotations may be found in J. M. and M. J. Cohen, *The Penguin Dictionary of Modern Quotations* (London: Penguin, 1971), *The Reader's Digest Treasury of Modern Quotations* (New York: Reader's Digest Press, 1975) (6,000 items), or James B. Simpson, *Simpson's Contemporary Quotations* (Boston: Houghton Mifflin, 1988). Among many dictionaries of Latin phrases, foreign language phrases, and Latin legal phrases, some of the best are listed in Anthony W. Shipps, *The Quote Sleuth: A Manual for the Tracer of Lost Quotations* (Urbana, Ill., and Chicago: University of Illinois Press, 1990). Often the quickest route lies through ordinary dictionaries, indexes, or footnote references: for these and other ways of finding directions out by indirections, Shipps is an excellent guide.

If you are looking for facts rather than words, start with such miscellaneous compilations as David Crystal's *The Cambridge Factfinder* (1993 etc.) or yearbooks such as *Whitaker's Almanack* and *Statesman's Yearbook*. But such works have a way of omitting just the information you need; and even Google and other search engines may fail. When you have to cast your net wider, research guides might help. I mentioned Barzun in the previous chapter, and Harner. Here may be added Mona McCormick, *The New York Times Guide to Reference Materials* (1979); and James D. Lester, *Writing Research Papers: A Complete Guide* (1980).

For facts about individuals, try *Who's Who; Who's Who in America; Who Was Who; Oxford Dictionary of National Biography* (40 vols., 2004); *Dictionary of American Biography; Dictionary of Scientific Biography; Biography Index* (1947–); *Encyclopedia of American Biography; New York Times Obituary Index*; professional directories; and encyclopedias (the *New Encyclopedia Britannica* has an electronic version). For British authors, consult first *The New Cambridge Bibliography of English Literature*, 5 vols. (1969–77), then the old but still very useful S. Austin Allibone and John Foster Kirk, *Critical Dictionary of English Literature and British and American Authors*, 5 vols. (1859–92). Authors figure in the many companions to literature, such as Henry and Mary Garland's *The Oxford Companion to German Literature* (1976) or Gordon Campbell's *Oxford Dictionary of the Renaissance* (2003), and there are Cambridge Companions to some individual authors. Many institutions publish annual calendars giving names of those currently holding office; for historical officeholders consult *Handbook of British Chronology*, ed. E. B. Fryde et al., 3rd edn. (London: Royal Historical Society, 1986). Or there is Patrick Hanks et al., *The Oxford Names Companion* (2002) (70,000 surnames) and B. E. Smith, *The Century Cyclopedia of Names*, rev. edn. (New York: Century, 1911) (over 60,000 names). The *Monthly Catalog of United States*

Government Publications runs from 1895; and the *International Index to Periodicals* from 1907 (although it is not very international).

Ideas, books, and special areas of knowledge can be harder to locate. Begin with a research guide, and go on to progressively more specialized bibliographies. For literature, and to some extent history, there are *The New Cambridge Bibliography of English Literature* (*NCBEL*); *The Oxford Chronology of English Literature* (unreliable, with large omissions); and the appendixes to *The Oxford History of English Literature* (12 vols; 1945–90); the *Oxford English Literary History* (13 vols; 2002–); and the *New Cambridge History of English Literature* (1999–).

Other areas have their own bibliographical aids, such as Blanche Henrey, *British Botanical and Horticultural Literature Before 1800*, 3 vols. (1975); *The Oxford Guide to Classical Mythology in the Arts, 1300–1990*, 2 vols. (1993); and *The New Grove Dictionary of Music and Musicians*, ed. Stanley Sadie, 20 vols. (1980). And you can search online the catalogues of the British Library, the Bodleian Library, and some others.

If you have to make an exhaustive search, there are bibliographies of bibliographies, for example F. Toomey, *A World Bibliography of Bibliographies 1964–1974*, 2 vols. (1977). Search engines will not help with exhaustive searching, since they do not venture far into the past. So you have to go through annual volumes such as *The Year's Work in English Studies; Annual Bibliography of English Language and Literature* (1920–); and *The MLA International Bibliography* (1956–) (again, not fully international).

24. Practicalities

Writers are generally averse to rules; when critics imposed prescriptive dogmas in the eighteenth century, the unruly freeflow of Romanticism ensued. Every sort of writing pattern suits someone: some write on-screen from start to finish, while others never touch a keyboard; some write nocturnally for the silence; some don't write at all for months and then produce a book in a few manic days, regardless of their surroundings.

WHERE

The place that works for you may be anywhere. Some prefer an institutional library, others their own home (whether a study or a corner of the bedroom). Jane Austen used to write in company, Diana Wynne Jones with her notebook on the fridge out of reach of children. Writing in the presence of others may assuage the writer's loneliness, achieving concentration by heroic defiance of interruptions or supportive solidarity with the company. You can even write on a plane. Wherever it is, try to make the place habitual: some writers think it worthwhile for this to rent a room to write in, just for the regularity.

Most now assume that the normal posture for writing is seated. But after prolonged sitting, momentum flags: you can work longer if you write standing up, as Henry James points out in *The Lesson of the Master*. William Golding also used to write standing (for this, a ledger-clerk's desk is ideal). Whatever your posture, try to change it every fifteen minutes or so, to maximize blood circulation and maintain alertness. People of former generations wrote outdoors a good deal while they walked—Gibbon in a garden; Panofsky, as we saw, in the Princeton woods. Walking promotes rhythm in composition and tenacity in recollection. (If you have given up on memory there is always the voice-recorder.) But pedestrian composition has become harder, now that urban pavements are overrun with skateboards, roller-blades, and bicycles.

WHEN

However averse writers may be to rules, most of them find it useful to keep to a regular schedule. Starting in the morning, for example: experimental evidence shows that the main intellectual effort for the day is most effectively made before noon. As an old maxim has it, 'Morning is a friend to the Muses'. Writing (or trying to write) at more or less the same time each day will soon make the business less of a daunting, unnatural ordeal. It puts habit on your side.

WARMING UP

Writing, unlike the universe, doesn't come from nothing. (But, if the sight of a blank page makes you feel eager to go, skip this paragraph.) Many writers find it better to get going gradually: to ease gradually into the writing process rather than start from cold. Reading before writing seems a natural sequence of things; if you follow that plan, read something pleasurable, something that will take pressure off the heavy beginning. By all means read a manual about how to write ('he *would* say that'), but only a few sentences. Or you might look at a piece in the same genre that you're going to attempt—to get the feel of it and refresh your sense of its special language. If you keep a commonplace book, you could browse in that. And, if you have notes on the topic, you could go over them with a highlighter, to select passages for possible use. Working on-screen, you could cut-and-paste selected notes into a new file.

Perhaps you're in luck, and left the last few sentences of yesterday's draft unfinished: if so you can easily pick up the threads for a quick start. Otherwise, read over yesterday's stint to ensure continuity. When you're working on more than one project, try to arrange that they're out of step, so you can draft one in the morning and key the other later.

Some people jump-start the day's writing with letters or email, to get distractions out of the way. But on this point practices vary widely: C. S. Lewis used to begin each day by answering letters; Walter Scott postponed it as long as he could hold guilt at bay, then gave over a whole day to correspondence. Something depends on how heavy the correspondence is, and on whether it has become an excuse to evade the writing challenge. Starting with email is not a particularly good idea: it side-tracks effort and easily leads to further interruptions. In academic writing, even looking up references for documentation can lose momentum. Better postpone footnotes until after you have made your main effort: you can insert the gist of a footnote within the text, leaving it to be completed later. If a great many notes are called for, you can work out a routine of switching between text window and note panel.

Ideally you should write every day, whether on your main project or on short pieces. If that seems insuperably difficult, you clearly need to put more effort into making the act of writing a more ordinary, familiar activity. Keeping a private journal or commonplace book may help. A commonplace book can build many writing skills: the critic Edmund Wilson, for example, used to enlarge his descriptive resources by collecting depictions of landscape. Or, if you have the time, writing exercises are good practice: try manipulating a paragraph by expanding it, contracting it, rewriting it (as the words of a lunatic, say, or a politician). The same paragraph can be made formal, informal, sensuous, nostalgic, farouche.

When you have finished a section in readable draft, you might show it to friends or colleagues to get feedback. But when you do this take care not to talk your ideas out and lose some of the pressure to express yourself in writing. The danger of having ideas stolen is usually unreal; but the fear of it can easily arouse anxiety.

MATERIALS

Never let yourself run out of writing materials; shortages can be inhibiting beyond all proportion. Writers avoid this problem in very different ways. Some (of whom I am one) always have an abundance of materials ready to hand—a superfluity, in fact; others are happy to draft on the back of a used envelope, a bus ticket, a computer screen, or anything else ready to hand. The frugality of cheap paper recommends it to some; to others an attractive paper is preferable (for many purposes, 80 grams photocopying paper serves well and is cheaper than typing paper). Some like ruled paper: it makes their writing neater, if not more legible; others prefer unruled paper, as allowing freedom of scale and placement. You will need writing surfaces of various sizes, from A4 down to index cards (3 × 5 ins. or 6 × 4). Small paper slips are useful for drafting phrases or sentences; they can be laid on top of a passage on a larger sheet without hiding much of the content. Slips are also convenient as a temporary surface for notes to be inserted later. They can be cut from the foot of letters, combining frugality with the luxuriousness of expensive notepaper. Much the quickest way to cut slips is with an OLO cutter: one of these invaluable instruments should be at every work station.

ORDERING PAPERS

To hold cards and slips securely in order, you need thin elastic bands (7.5 mm) or jubilee clips or foldback clips (18 mm for a few slips, up to 40 mm for a large stack). Foldback clips are best for semi-permanent use, but the quickest and most efficient temporary holder is a large plastic clip of the clothes-peg type. Paper clips are cheap but dangerous: they easily come loose or (worse) pick up papers that belong elsewhere. For filing papers between writing sessions a transparent plastic display envelope is most convenient: the sort with two sides closed works best and costs relatively little if bought by the hundred.

To keep track of slips or cards you will require a labelling system. A number or letter in the top corner (always the same corner) can be keyed to a place in the draft: an insert labelled *3g* (meaning 'insert *g* for page 3') would go on page 3 at a place marked '*g*'. Alternatively a single slip can simply be stapled in place. If the inserts are very numerous, however, they will need to be ordered in a sorting tray or card file box. In all these orderly arrangements, beware: an elaborate system can take up excessive time and displace the primary work of writing. This is especially true of notes kept on the computer.

WRITING INSTRUMENTS

Almost any computer will do for editing text: capacity and speed are no longer important considerations to a writer. The days are long gone when it was necessary to split a book into short documents; modern computers can handle large texts quickly (a speed of 800 MHz is perfectly adequate), saving automatically every ten minutes or so. You can save, and even archive, on 3.5-in. floppy disks or on zip disks (100 or 250 Mb), but CDs (700 Mb) are now standard. Computing capacity and speed need only concern you if you have occasion to use very large databases. The *OED* on CD-ROM calls merely for a 200 MHz Pentium-class processor with 64 MB RAM and (installed on your hard disk) 1.7 GB space.

Choice of monitor, on the other hand, makes a great difference to the writer: go for a flat screen with high resolution, as high as you can afford. Then choose, via your processor, the standard option of white characters with blue background. The more contrasty black on white is less kind to the eyes.

Printers are now relatively inexpensive, so you can aim for a very good one, perhaps from the HP Laserjet 2000 series. Keyboards are cheaper still: demand the best. Some find the 'natural' keyboard more comfortable; but remember you may have to switch between it and the standard keyboard usual in libraries and on laptops—an adjustment not easy for touch-typists.

If you like mice, get an intelligent one. But editing by keystrokes is quicker for many purposes, particularly to those who touch-type.

Most people write either with a pen or a pencil, few with both. Pencil marks can be erased, but pencils must be kept sharp. Some writers keep a jar of pencils ready sharpened, as Kingsley Amis did; others find the sharpening a welcome break.

In a sense any pen will do (fountain, cartridge, gel, etc.), so long as it doesn't blot. But it pays the writer to select a pen carefully: a cheap ballpoint may seem to write perfectly well over the short haul but be slow over the distance. If your hand hurts after you have written continuously for an hour, try a thicker or thinner pen, or consider the type of pen with a shaft that moulds to the shape of your fingers. For writing a first draft speed matters a good deal, so that at that stage a soft nib or ball may be best. (The Pilot refill writes well, or the Fisher, or the Goliath from Manufactum.) For making corrections you will need a contrasting ink colour, perhaps a red Pilot Hi-Tecpoint 5.

Many think it is good enough to hunt and peck with one or two fingers on their keyboard, or even just a thumb. It is not. You can learn to touch-type properly in a few weeks; soon after that you will be as quick as a professional typist, although not, of course, so accurate (given a computer, accurate typing hardly matters, correction is so easy). When you edit a heavily corrected draft, you will find it more efficient (and more pleasant) to key the piece afresh. When processing quotations, too, keying is better than scanning—unless the passage is very long indeed.

Young writers and designers tend to prefer small font sizes, as presenting a more attractive image. But image is not everything: efficiency matters too, and 8-point or 10-point sizes can be laborious to readers with bad eyesight—as well as to most readers over 45 years old, who are (remember) the majority. The 12-point size of a readable font such as Times New Roman is a good compromise: older writers can edit it most efficiently when zoomed to about 150 per cent.

25. Recapitulation

In this book I try to meet the needs of so many different sorts of writers—students, graduate students, mature students, beginners, and professional people—that I can't possibly issue a single prescription for all. Yet it seems many would-be writers run into much the same difficulties. Not all of these arise from faulty education: some who know a good deal of grammar still struggle to write, and so have come to dislike writing. But if you have read the previous chapters you will agree, I hope, that anyone following the procedures they describe should be able to write at will. At least you will know how to solve the problem of getting started.

My main theme is that writing, far from being a single action, is normally a sequence of related steps, phases, activities. Few people can sit down to a blank page and simply write: most have to come to terms with a series of distinct processes: reading, note-taking, planning, outlining, drafting, revising, and addressing a readership. Instead of starting with words (usually a mistake), I have recommended postponing word choices until later—until the larger compositional elements (paragraphs, sentences, formulas) have been roughed out. In short, I advocate drafting rather than writing.

When a writer does begin to choose words and word forms, many complicated factors come into play. It isn't at all a matter of obeying a single set of rules: I've tried to look at different sorts of correctness (grammatical, aesthetic, political) in the perspective of current trends in the language. On such issues I am a moderate stickler: I think linguistic change can't be ignored but needn't be accelerated unnecessarily.

I offer this book merely as an elementary, practical guide, which may put you in a position to learn more about writing for yourself. It will at least palliate some of the agonies of composition, and may even change them into pleasures.

Further Reading

Amis, Kingsley, *The King's English: A Guide to Modern Usage* (London: Harper Collins, 1997). Combative but mostly sensible.

Beard, Henry, and Cerf, Christopher, *The Official Politically Correct Dictionary and Handbook* (London: Grafton, 1992). An all too complete account of PC language.

Bierce, Ambrose, *Write It Right: A Little Blacklist of Literary Faults* (New York: Neale, 1909). The faults detected are sometimes over-subtle by modern standards.

Burchfield, Robert, *The New Fowler's Modern English Usage* (Oxford: Oxford University Press, 1996). The best guide to current usage.

Cochrane, James, *Between You and I: A Little Book of Bad English* (Cambridge: Icon, 2003). Lists contemporary errors.

Crystal, David, *Rediscover Grammar* (London: Longman, 1988).

—— *The Cambridge Encyclopedia of the English Language* (Cambridge: Cambridge University Press, 1995). Up-to-date account of grammar, among much else. Good for browsing in.

—— *Language and the Internet* (Cambridge: Cambridge University Press, 2001). Explores influences of computer use on the language.

Dent, Susie, *The Language Report* (Oxford: Oxford University Press, 2003). Chronicles new words and tendencies; like Smith, but more powerful.

Elbow, Peter, *Everyone Can Write: Essays Toward a Hopeful Theory of Writing and Teaching Writing* (New York: Oxford

University Press, 2000). Wise reflections on a lifetime of composition teaching.

Gaskell, Philip, *Standard Written English: A Guide* (Edinburgh: Edinburgh University Press, 1998). Sound but all too brief introduction to the idea of a written standard.

Gowers, Sir Ernest, *The Complete Plain Words*, rev. Sir Bruce Fraser (London: HMSO, 1973). A classic guide to choosing words.

Graves, Robert, and Hodge, Alan, *The Reader over Your Shoulder: A Handbook for Writers of English Prose* (London: Cape, 1943). Salutary warnings against common faults, with many real-life examples.

Hicks, Wynford, *Quite Literally: Problem Words and How to Use Them* (London: Routledge, 2004). Identifies common blunders and cheapened words, more economically than Poerksen.

Kane, Thomas S., *The Oxford Guide to Writing* (New York: Oxford University Press, 1983). A successful textbook, with exercises.

Kaye, Sanford, *Writing under Pressure: The Quick Writing Process* (Oxford: Oxford University Press, 1989). A practical game-plan for writing against the clock.

Kramarae, Cheris, and Treichler, Paula, *A Feminist Dictionary* (Boston and London: Pandora, 1985). Likely to surprise, and perhaps infuriate, unreconstructed sexists.

Lanham, Richard A., *Analyzing Prose*, 2nd edn. (London and New York: Continuum, 2003). A rhetorical approach to prose style.

Manser, Martin, and Curtis, Stephen, *The Penguin Writer's Manual* (London: Penguin, 2002). Short and sensible.

Palmer, Frank, *Grammar* (London: Penguin, 1971). An elementary primer.

Partridge, Eric, *You Have a Point There*, rev. edn. (London:

Hamish Hamilton, 1964). The classic account of punctuation, now in need of updating.

Peters, Pam, *The Cambridge Guide to English Usage* (Cambridge: Cambridge University Press, 2004). Similar coverage to Burchfield's but with its own viewpoint.

Poerksen, Uwe, *Plastic Words: The Tyranny of a Modular Language*, tr. Jutta Mason and David Cayley (University Park, Pa.: Pennsylvania State University Press, 1995). Like Hicks, but giving fuller treatment of a few prevalent words that substitute for thought.

Quirk, Lord, et al., *A Comprehensive Grammar of the English Language* (London: Longman, 1985).

Rodari, Gianni, *The Grammar of Fantasy*, tr. Jack Zipes (New York: Teachers & Writers Collaborative, 1996). An original account of invention in writing.

Sellers, Leslie, *Doing it in Style: A Manual for Journalists, PR Men and Copywriters* (Oxford: Pergamon, 1968). Required reading for journalists.

Smith, Ken, *Junk English* (New York: Blast Books, 2001). Shrewd chronicle of current developments, but less concise than Dent.

Strunk, William, and White, E. B., *The Elements of Style*, 3rd edn. (New York: Macmillan; London: Collier Macmillan, 1979). Long-established elementary textbook, now out of date.

Truss, Lynne, *Eats, Shoots and Leaves: The Zero Tolerance Approach to Punctuation* (London: Profile, 2003). An amusing onslaught on contemporary sloppiness: mostly cogent but given to oversimplification.

Vallins, G. H., *Good English: How to Write It*, 5th edn. (London: Deutsch, 1955). A general treatment, fuller than Manser and Curtis.

Zinsser, William, *On Writing Well: An Informal Guide to*

Writing Nonfiction, 2nd edn. (New York: Harper & Row, 1980). An anecdotal approach to problems of writing by an experienced teacher and journalist.

Index